I0818099

Great-Grandmother Remembers

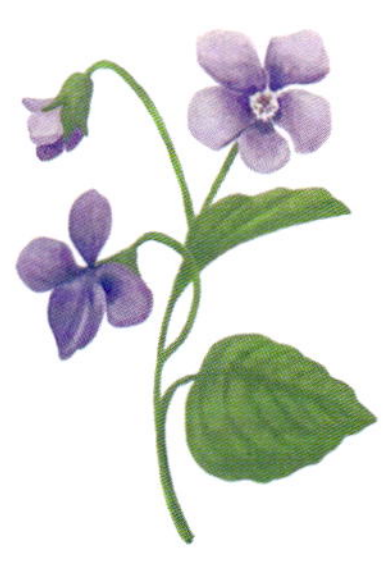

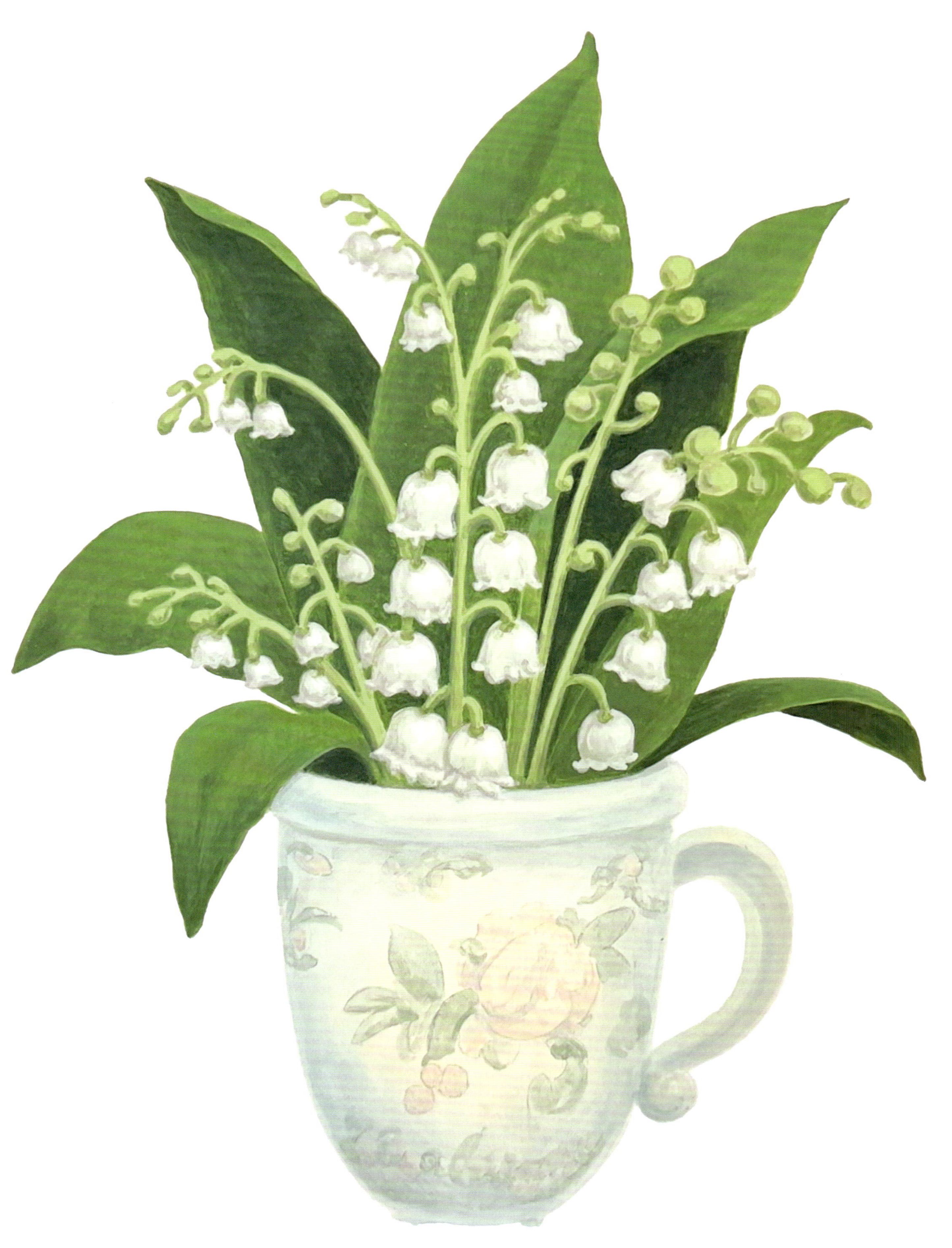

Great-Grandmother Remembers

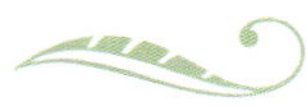

An Heirloom Treasury of Memories

Conceived and written by Judith Levy
Illustrated by Noelle Giddings

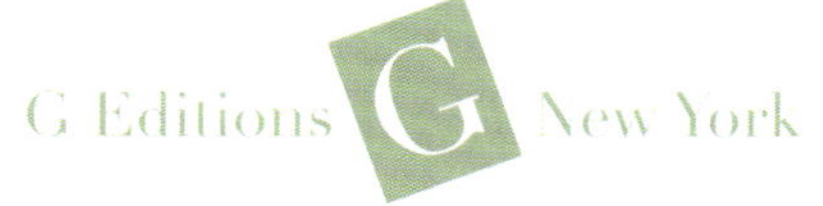

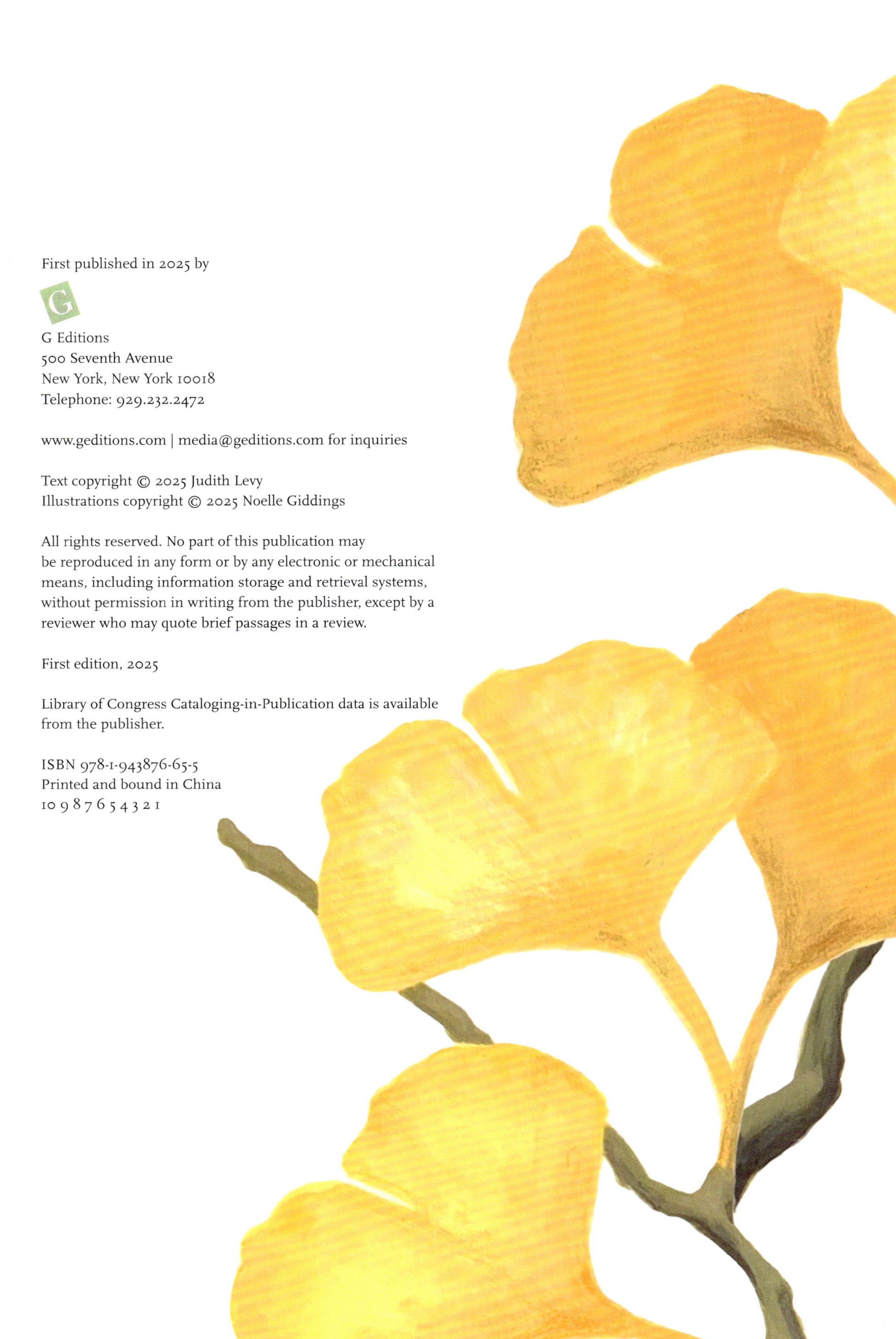

First published in 2025 by

G Editions
500 Seventh Avenue
New York, New York 10018
Telephone: 929.232.2472

www.geditions.com | media@geditions.com for inquiries

Text copyright © 2025 Judith Levy
Illustrations copyright © 2025 Noelle Giddings

All rights reserved. No part of this publication may be reproduced in any form or by any electronic or mechanical means, including information storage and retrieval systems, without permission in writing from the publisher, except by a reviewer who may quote brief passages in a review.

First edition, 2025

Library of Congress Cataloging-in-Publication data is available from the publisher.

ISBN 978-1-943876-65-5
Printed and bound in China
10 9 8 7 6 5 4 3 2 1

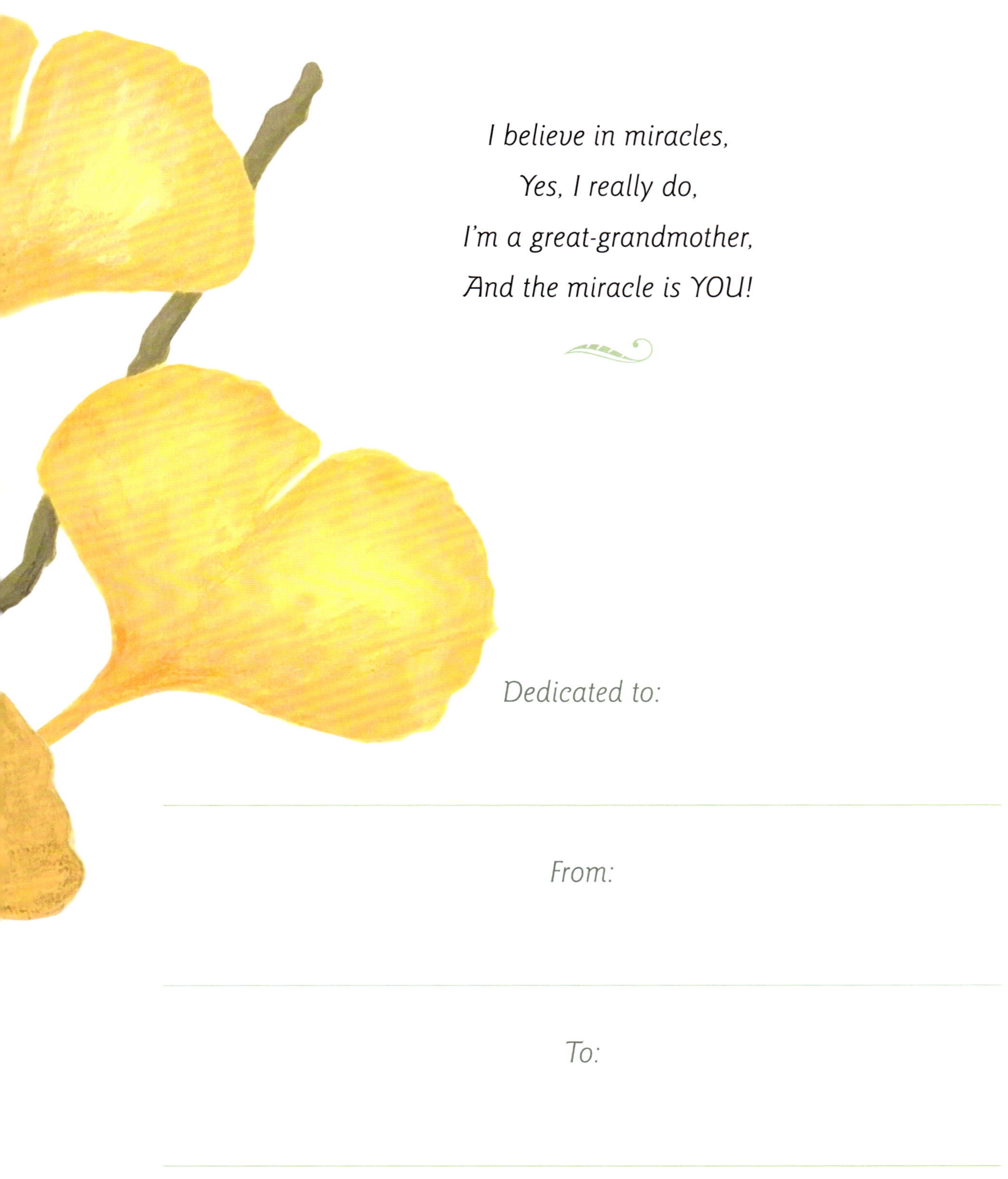

I believe in miracles,
Yes, I really do,
I'm a great-grandmother,
And the miracle is YOU!

Dedicated to:

From:

To:

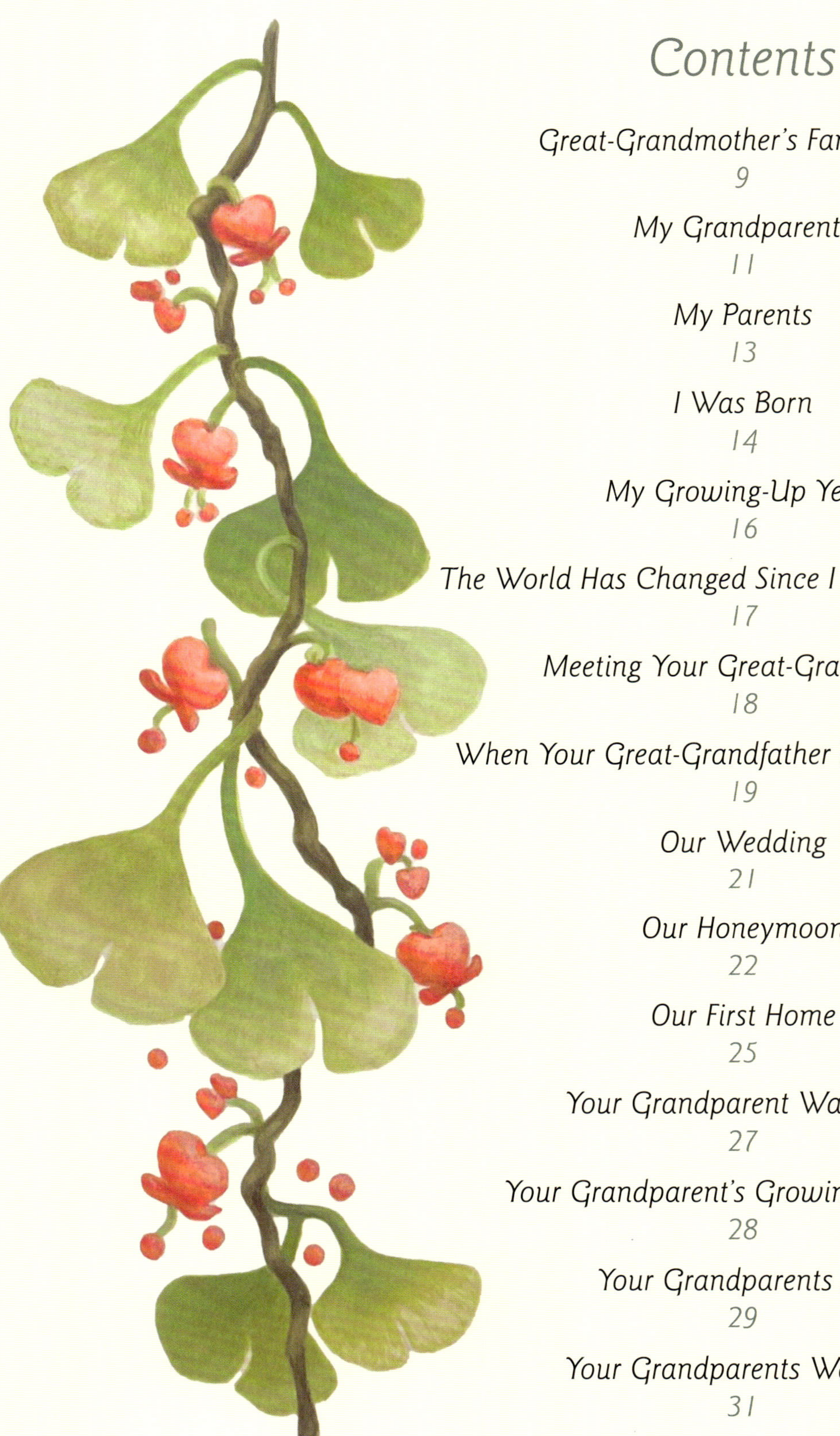

Contents

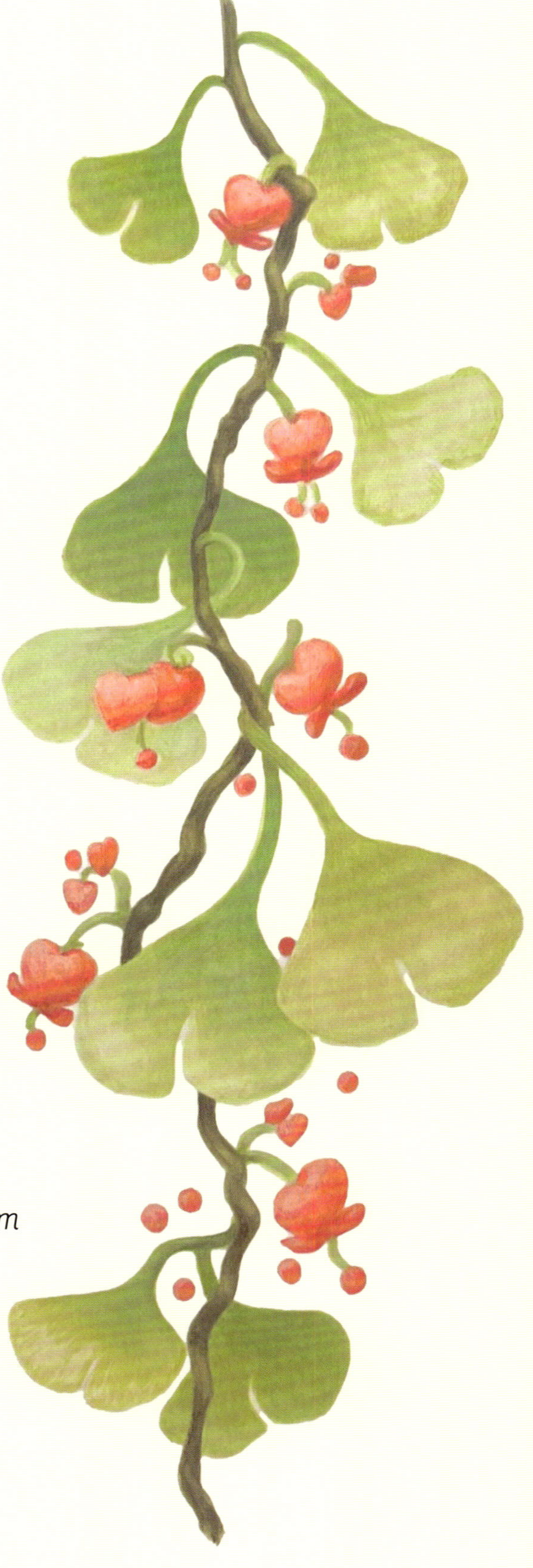

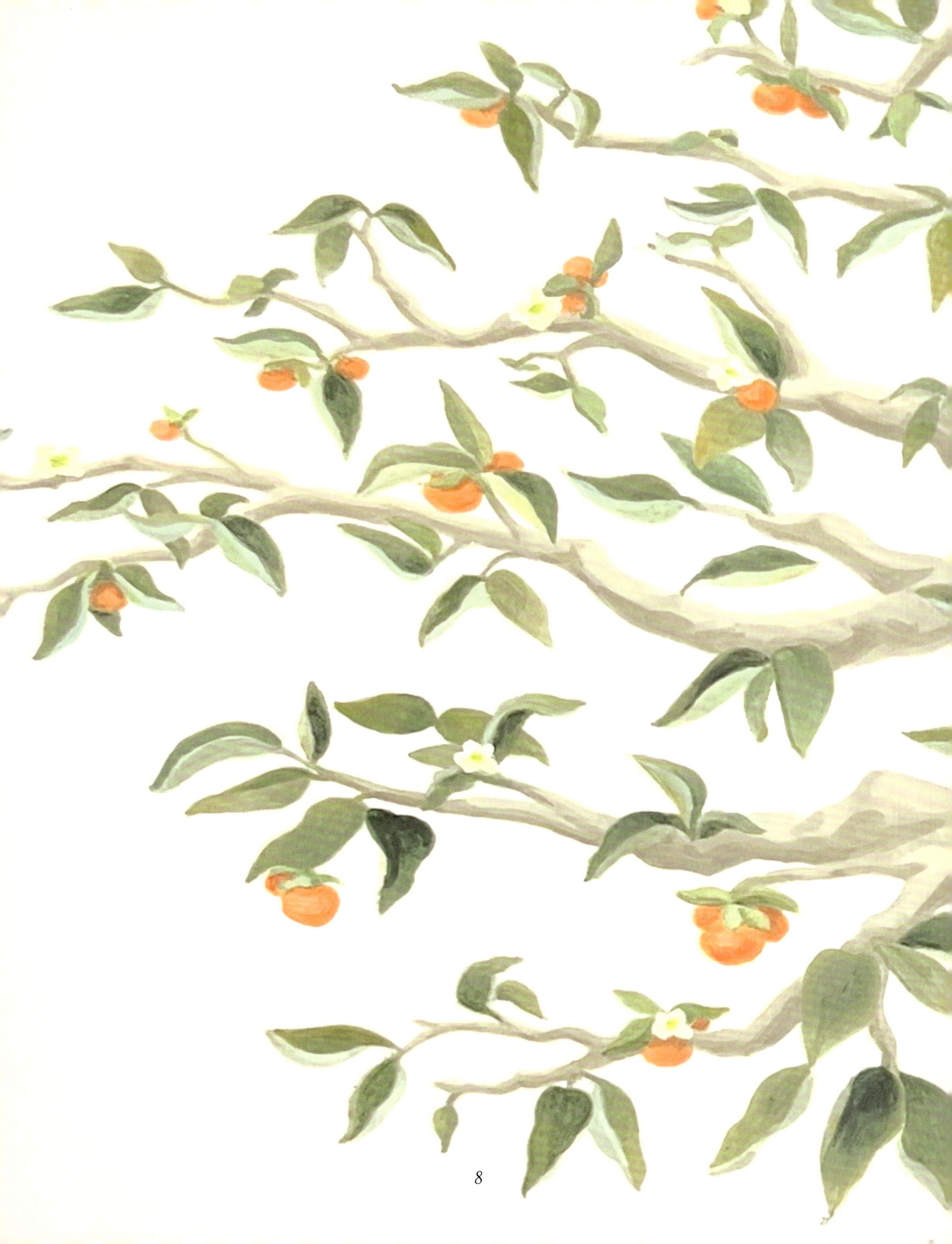

Great-Grandmother's Family Tree

So many branches,
I have lived to see,
We welcome you little one,
To our precious family tree.

_____________________ Great-Grandmother

_____________________ Great-Grandmother

_____________________ Great-Grandfather

_____________________ Great-Grandfather

_____________________ Great-Grandmother

_____________________ Great-Grandmother

_____________________ Great-Grandfather

_____________________ Great-Grandfather

_____________________ Grandmother

_____________________ Grandmother

_____________________ Grandfather

_____________________ Grandfather

_____________________ Mother

_____________________ Father

_____________________ Great-Grandchild

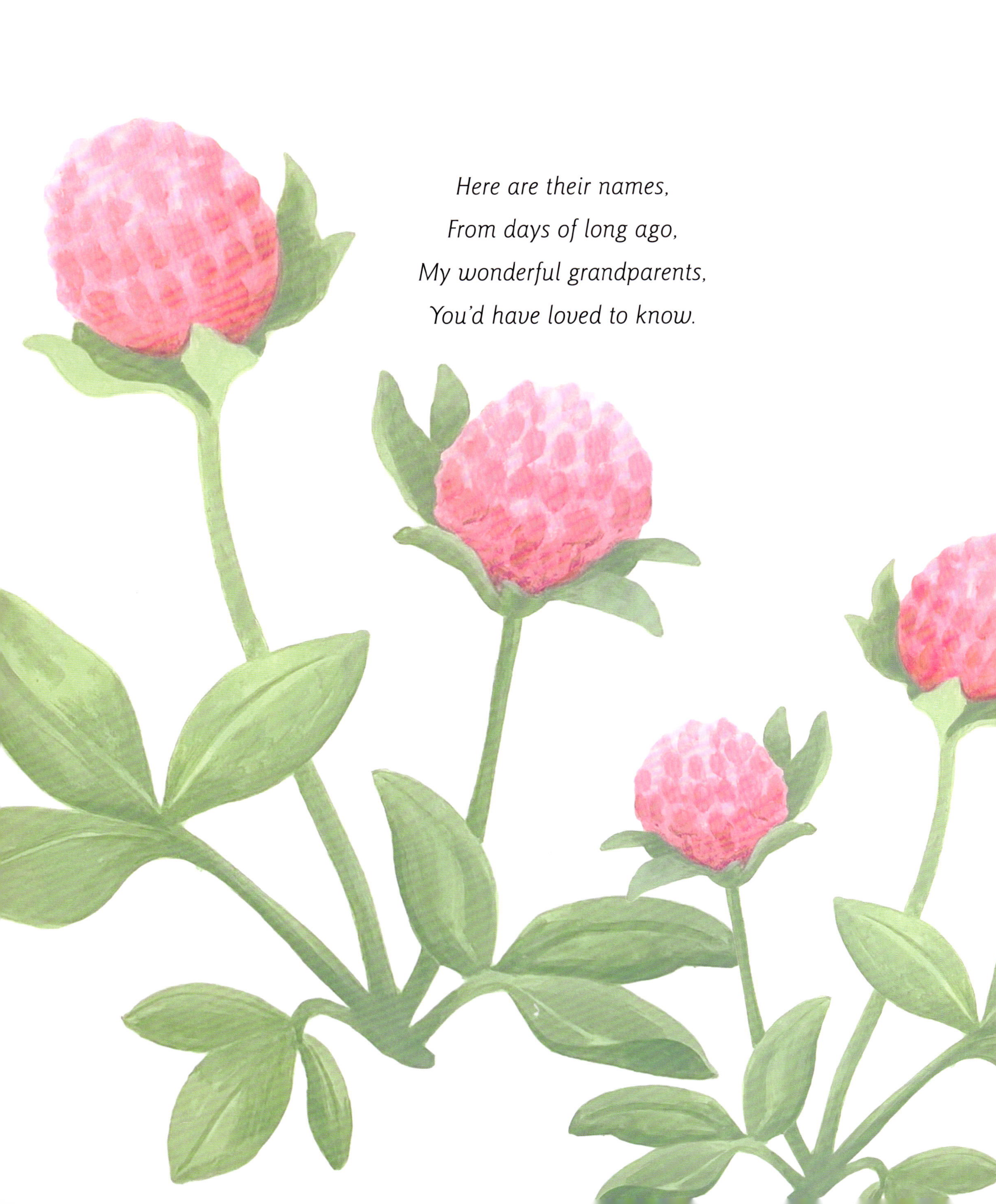

Here are their names,
From days of long ago,
My wonderful grandparents,
You'd have loved to know.

My Grandparents

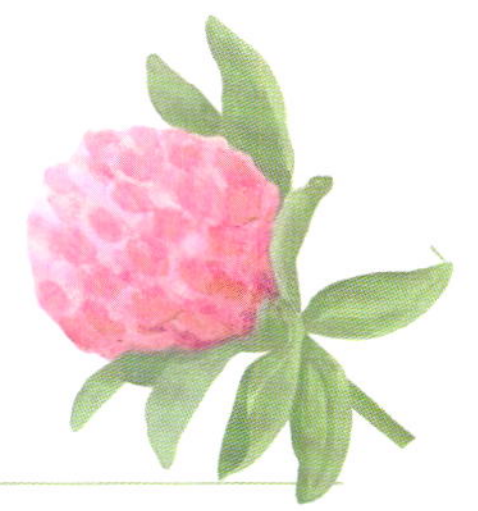

My maternal grandparents' names

They came from

My grandfather earned his living by

Their children's names

What I remember most about my grandparents

My paternal grandparents' names

They came from

My grandfather earned his living by

Their children's names

What I remember most about my grandparents

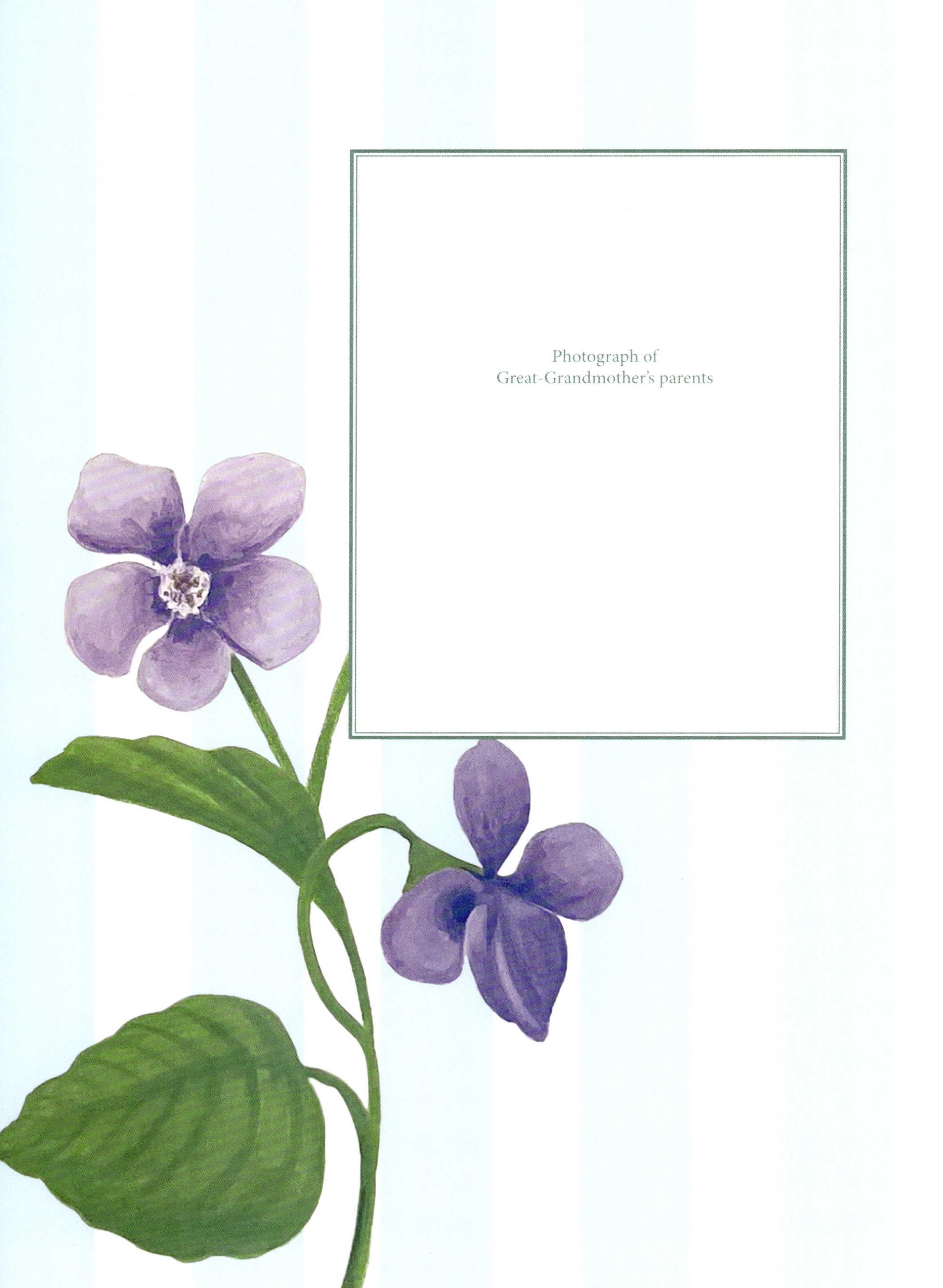

Photograph of
Great-Grandmother's parents

My Parents

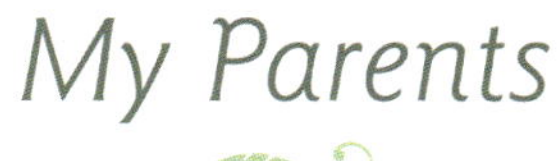

My parents taught me many things,
I remember to this day,
Just be a decent person,
And this is what they'd say.

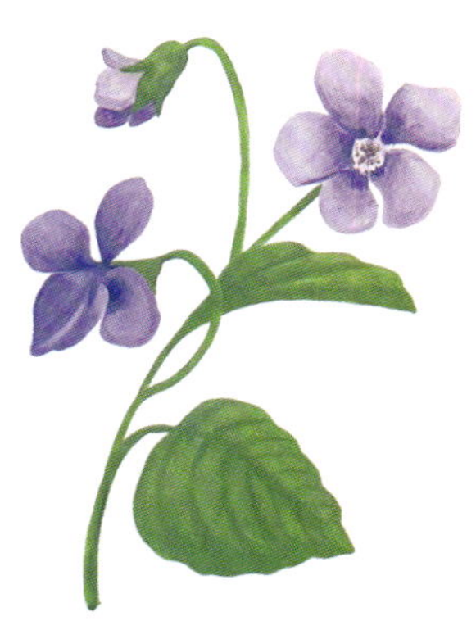

Make certain you help someone

If you've made a mistake, you should

Be forgiving and overlook

Be generous when

When you love someone, be sure you

I Was Born

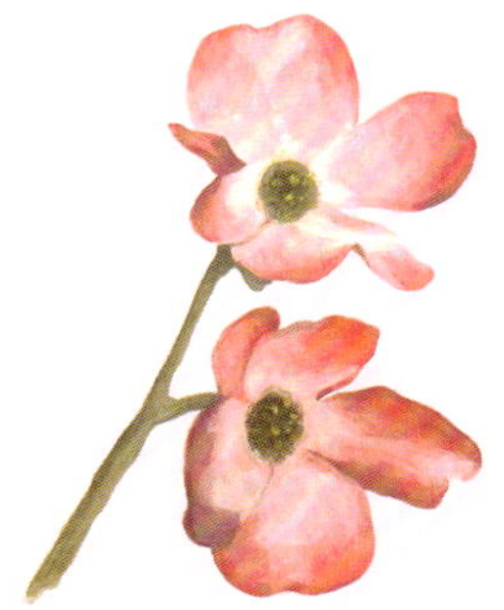

I don't remember very much,
I was little, as you know,
But here's what my parents told me
About what happened long ago.

The date of my birth

The place of my birth

I weighed

I was named

I was given that name because

We lived at

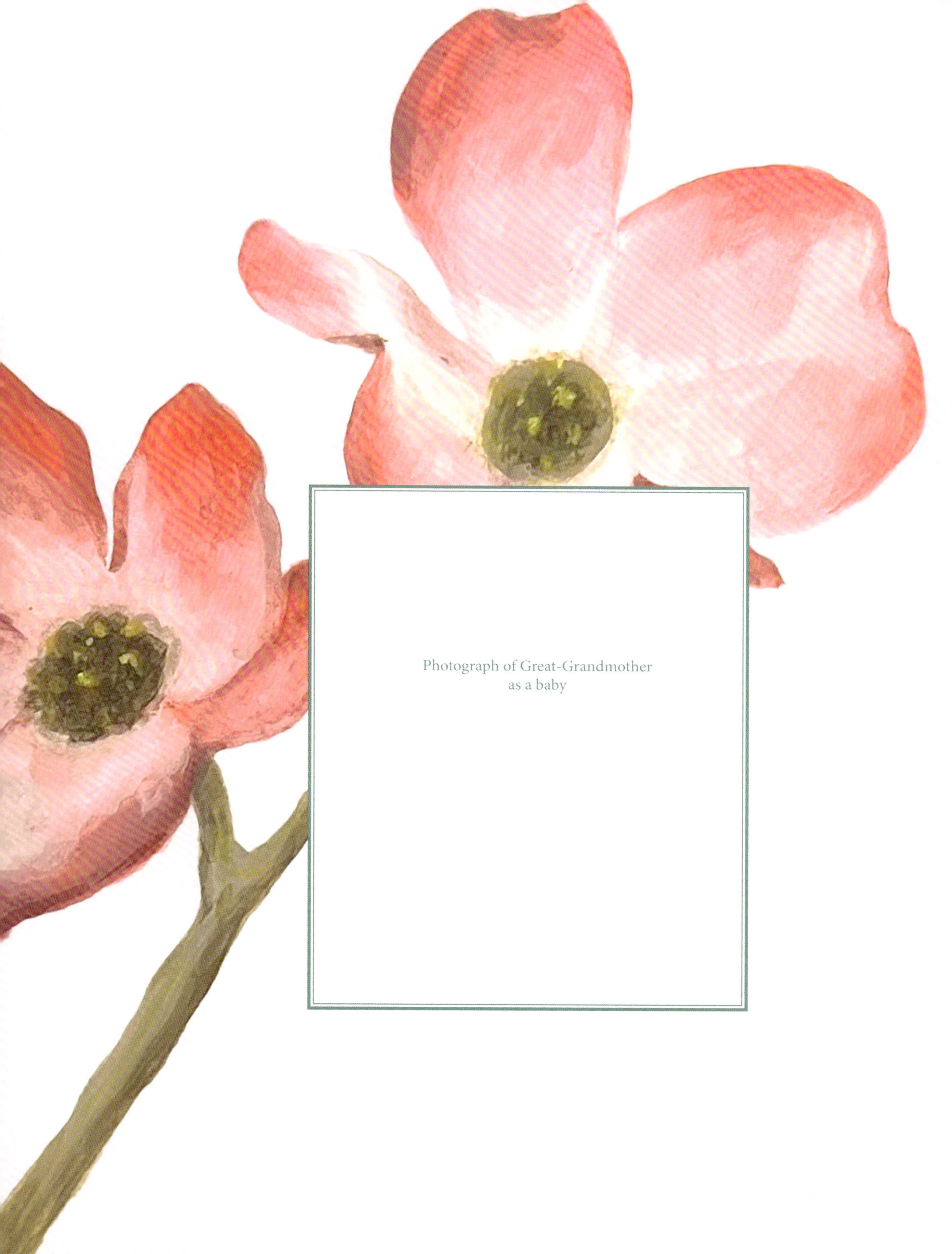
Photograph of Great-Grandmother
as a baby

My Growing-Up Years

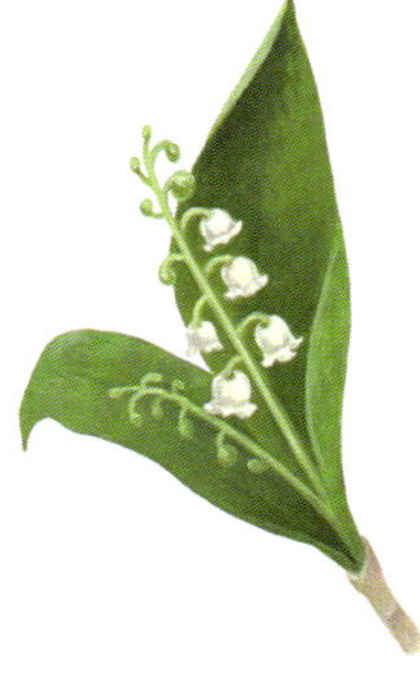

Things were very different then,
Not so much to do,
We were supposed to be polite,
And only speak when spoken to.

My elementary school(s)

My high school

My ambition

At home I was expected to

I didn't want to

I wanted to

The World Has Changed Since I Was a Little Girl

Who would have believed,
How so much came to be,
Brilliant minds came up with,
Such amazing discoveries!

They invented ______

They discovered ______

They came up with the cure for ______

Our car make and model was ______

Long before cell phones, we had party-line telephones and then ______

Meeting Your Great-Grandfather

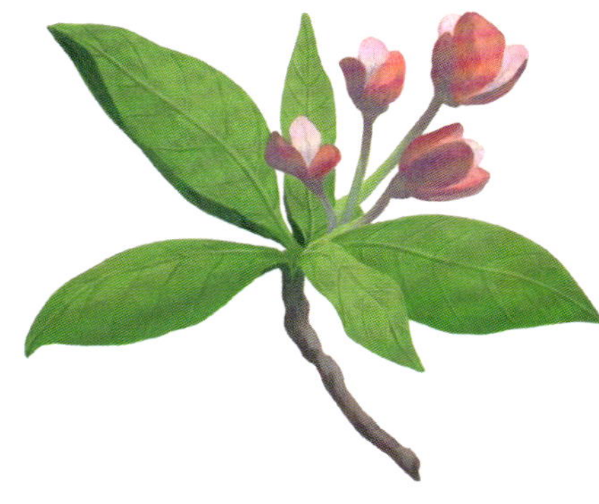

Meeting your great-grandfather,
Was so much fun,
Of all the men in the world,
I knew he was the one.

I met your great-grandfather at ______________________

____

____

Our courtship lasted for ______________________

____

My parents thought he was ______________________

____

____

His education included ______________________

____

____

He earned his living by ______________________

____

____

I was in love with him because ______________________

____

____

____

When Your Great-Grandfather Proposed to Me

Did he get down on his knee?
No, instead he just said,
He loved me very much,
And wanted us to wed.

When he proposed, he said

Of course, I said

Where it happened

I was thrilled because

The ring he gave me was

I couldn't wait to show it off to

The first person I told was

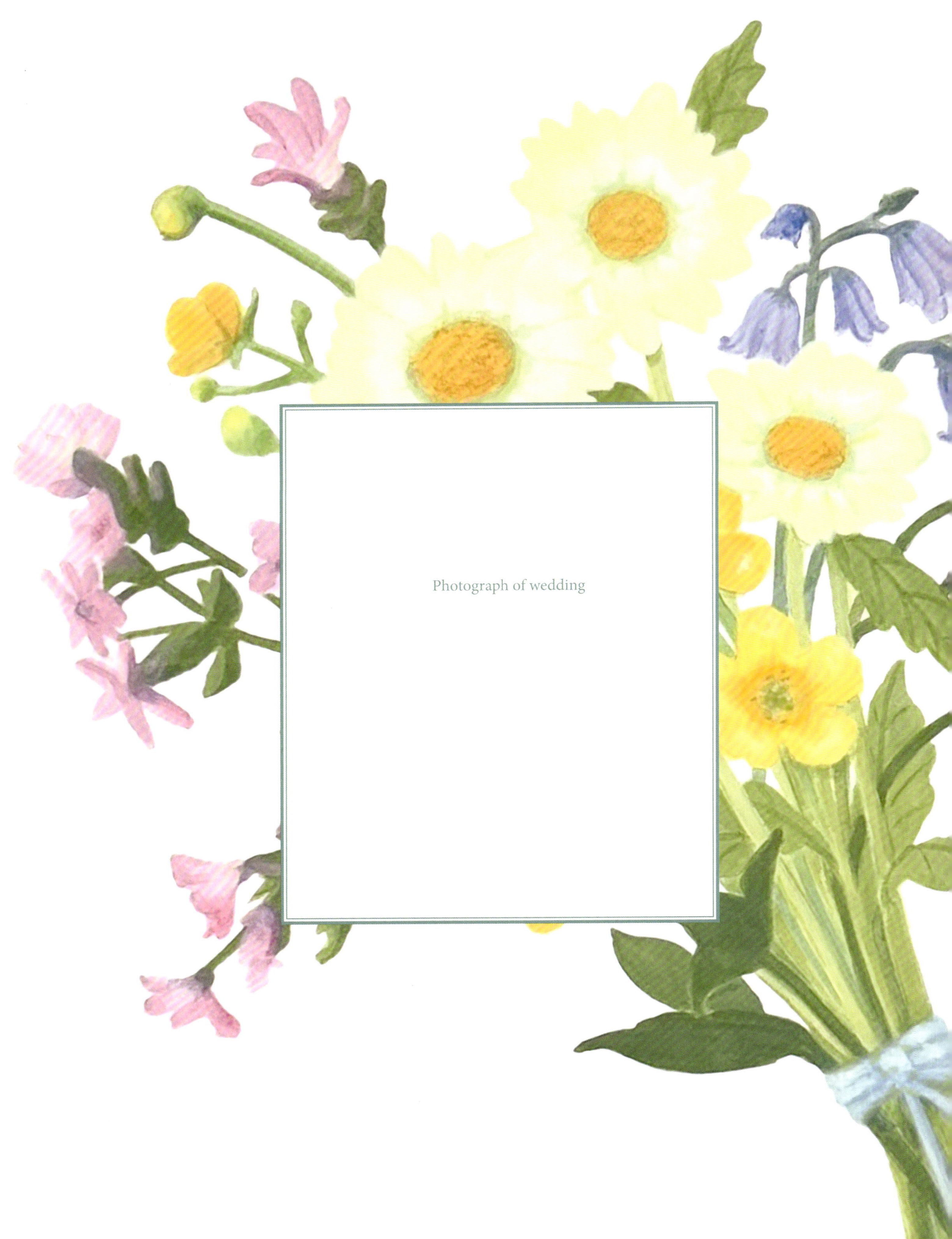

Photograph of wedding

Our Wedding

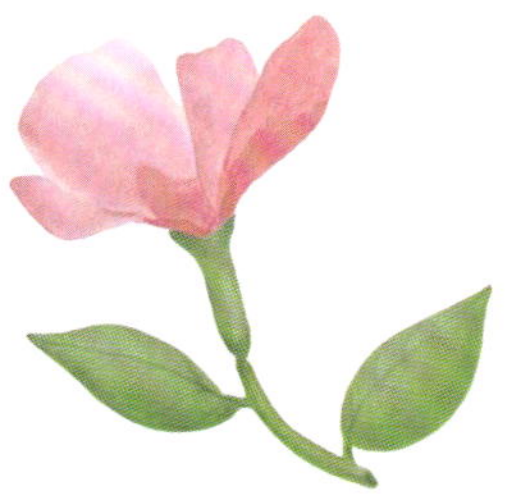

I was dressed so prettily,
When I walked down the aisle,
My groom was waiting for me,
With such a happy smile.

We were married at ______________________

____

Date ______________________

____

Our wedding party included ______________________

____

____

Our guests were ______________________

____

____

____

We served ______________________

____

____

Our song ______________________

____

My fondest memory of our wedding ______________________

____

____

____

Our Honeymoon

Our honeymoon was special,
The place, the food, and such,
A time to remember,
Because we loved so much.

For our honeymoon, we went to

We stayed for

The weather was

Souvenirs I brought home were

What I remember most about that special time

Photograph of honeymoon

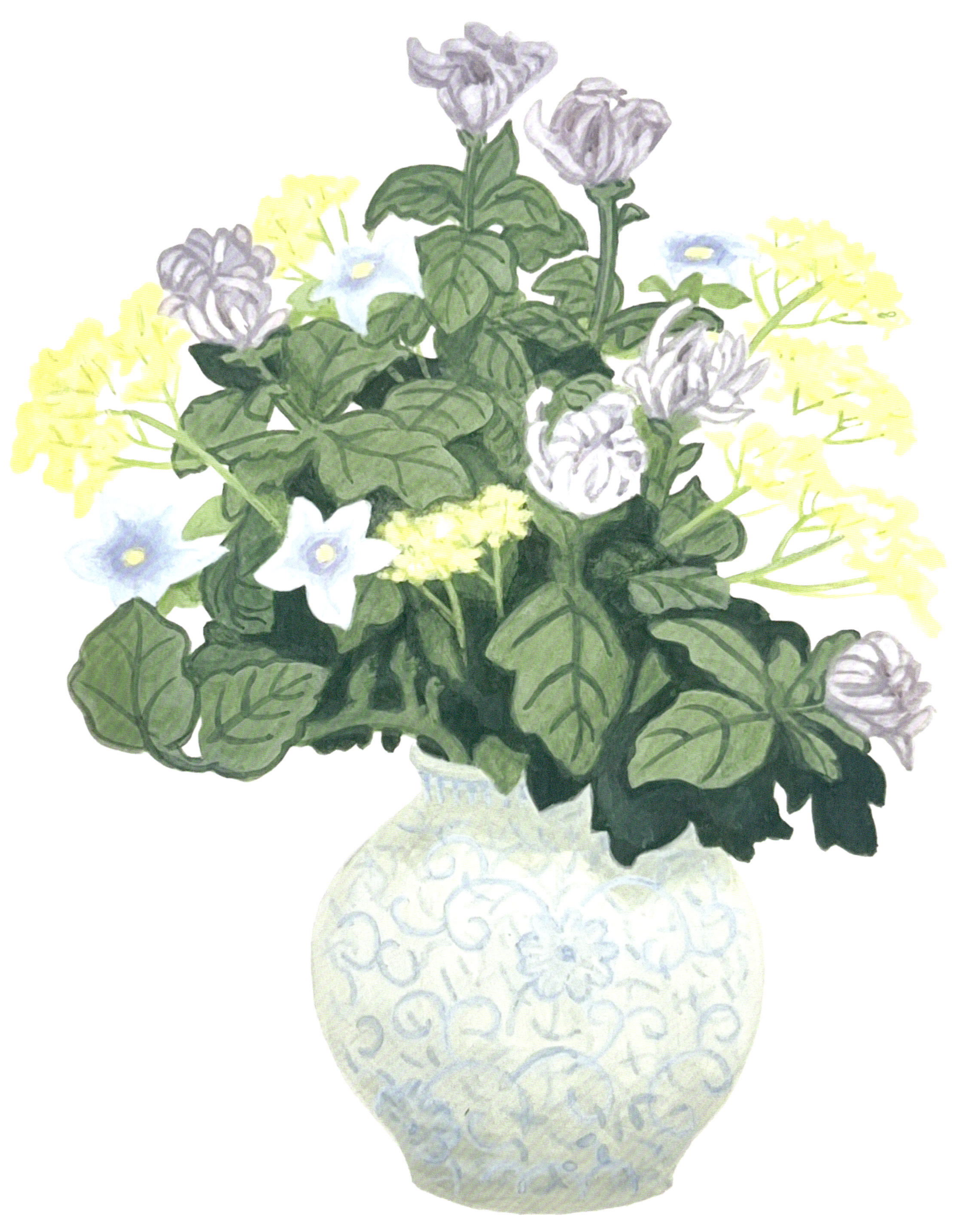

Our First Home

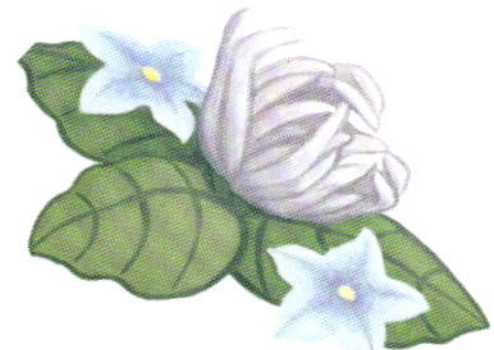

Should we rent or should we buy?
We could not decide,
It was a big decision,
For a new bridegroom and bride.

Our home was located at ______________________________

____

____

The years that we lived there ______________________________

____

Our new friends and neighbors were ______________________________

____

____

____

____

____

We enjoyed our home because ______________________________

____

____

____

____

____

____

____

When our baby was born,
Happiness came our way,
There's something about a baby's smile,
That brightens every day.

Photograph of Grandparent as a baby

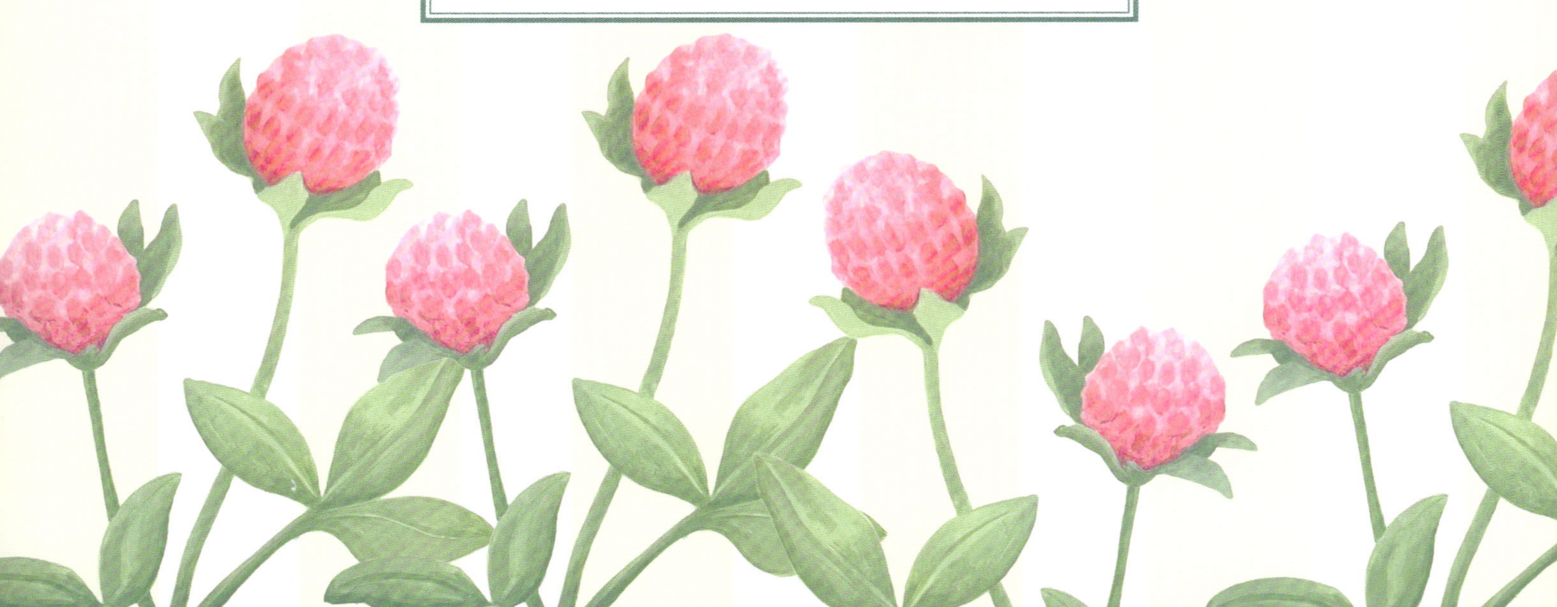

Your Grandparent Was Born

Our child was born on

We named the baby

That name was given because

We celebrated the birth of our child by

Our guests were

We were so excited because

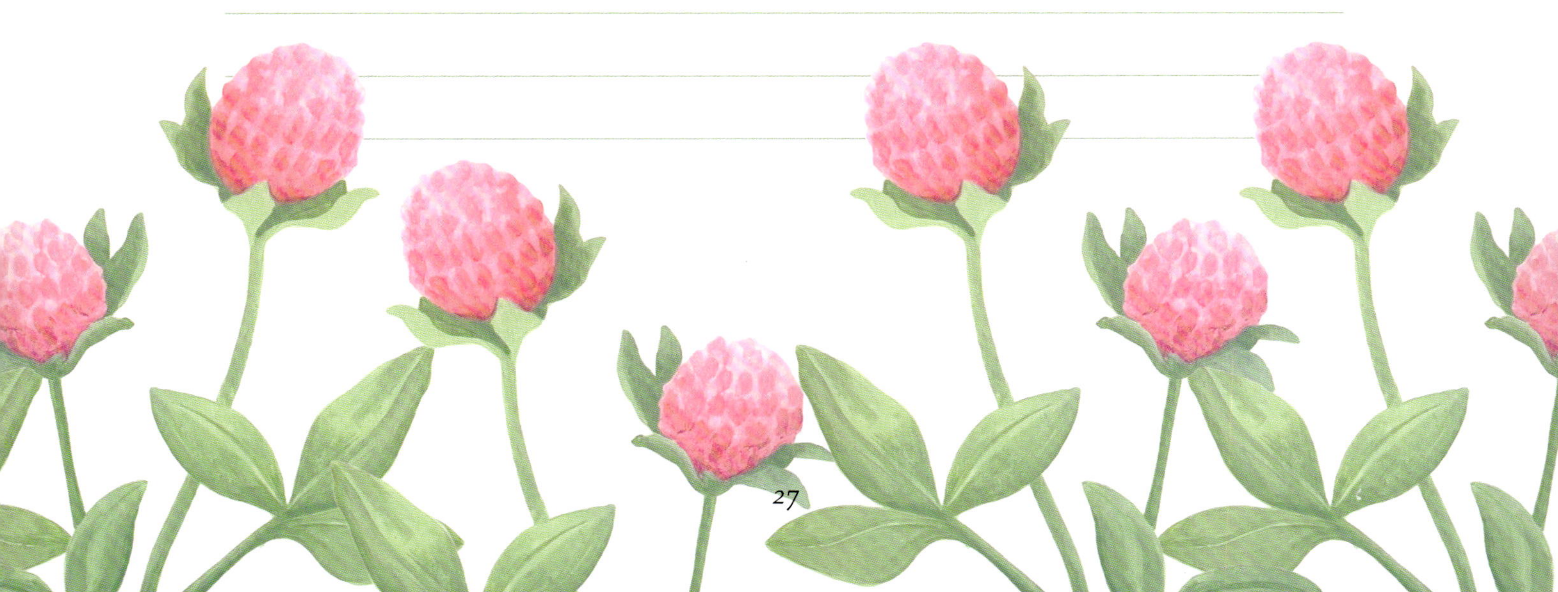

Your Grandparent's Growing Up Years

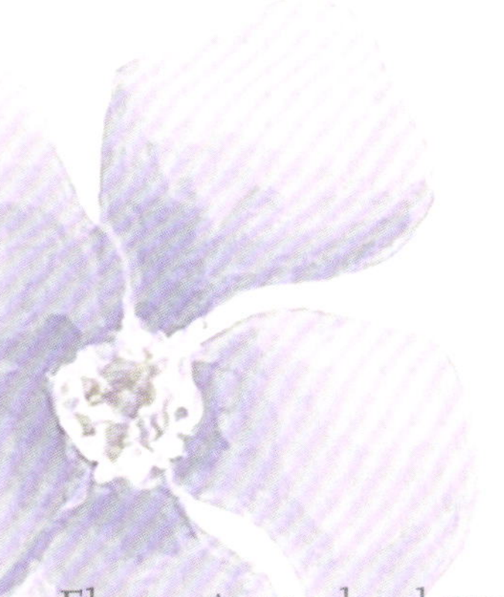

My child grew up quickly,
The years just flew away,
Lots of school and fun,
Then it was graduation day.

Elementary school was

My child excelled in

When it came to sports

Their ambitions were

After high school

When it came to college

Your Grandparents Met

It was interesting how they met,
And how they fell in love,
I think it was destiny,
Sent from up above.

They first met ______________________________

____

____

____

They dated for ______________________________

____

____

They were a good couple because ______________________________

____

____

____

My hopes for their future were ______________________________

____

____

____

We wanted the best for them because ______________________________

____

____

____

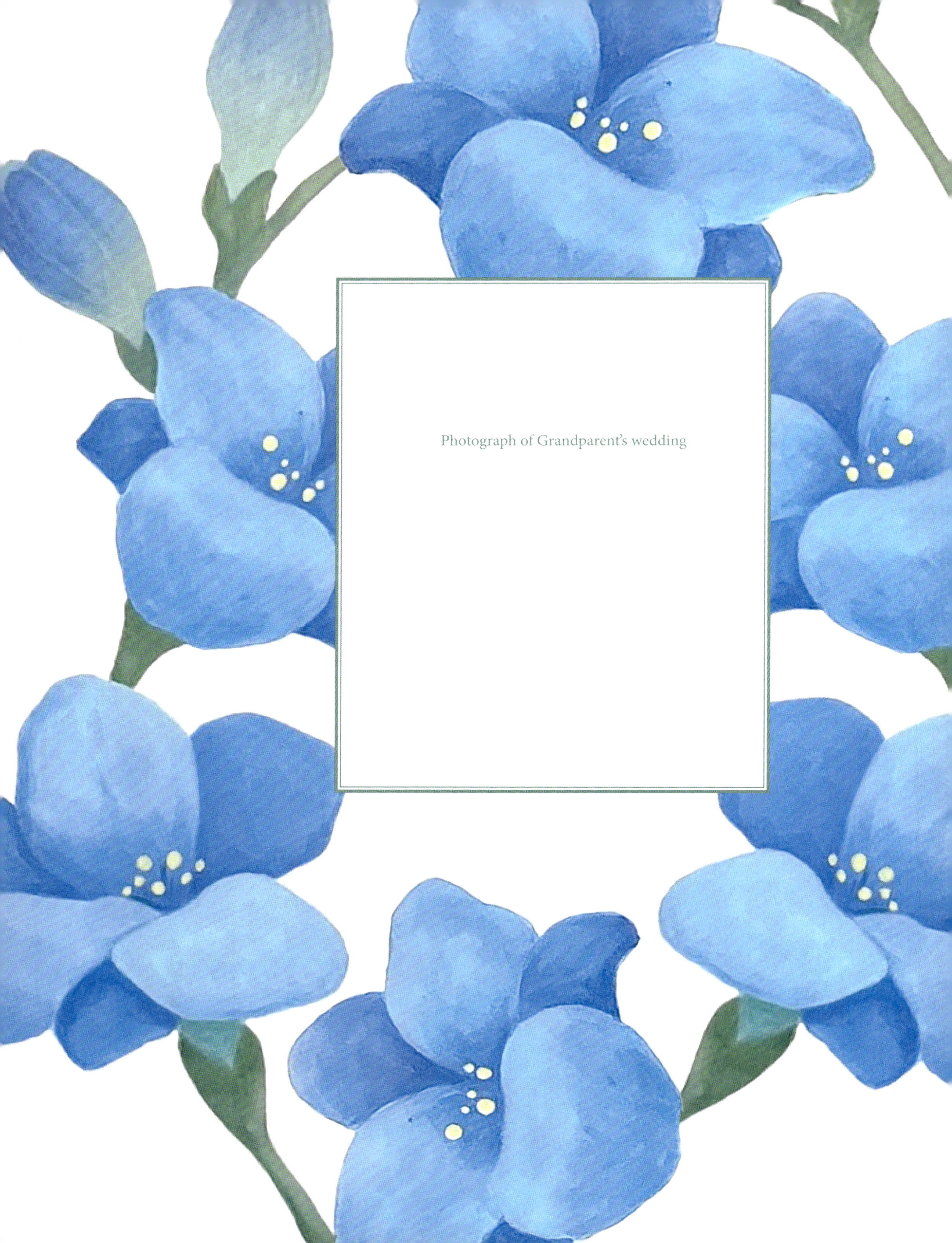
Photograph of Grandparent's wedding

Your Grandparents' Wedding

Our hearts were filled with joy,
When we heard "Here Comes the Bride"
Our happiness was complete,
As the knot was tied.

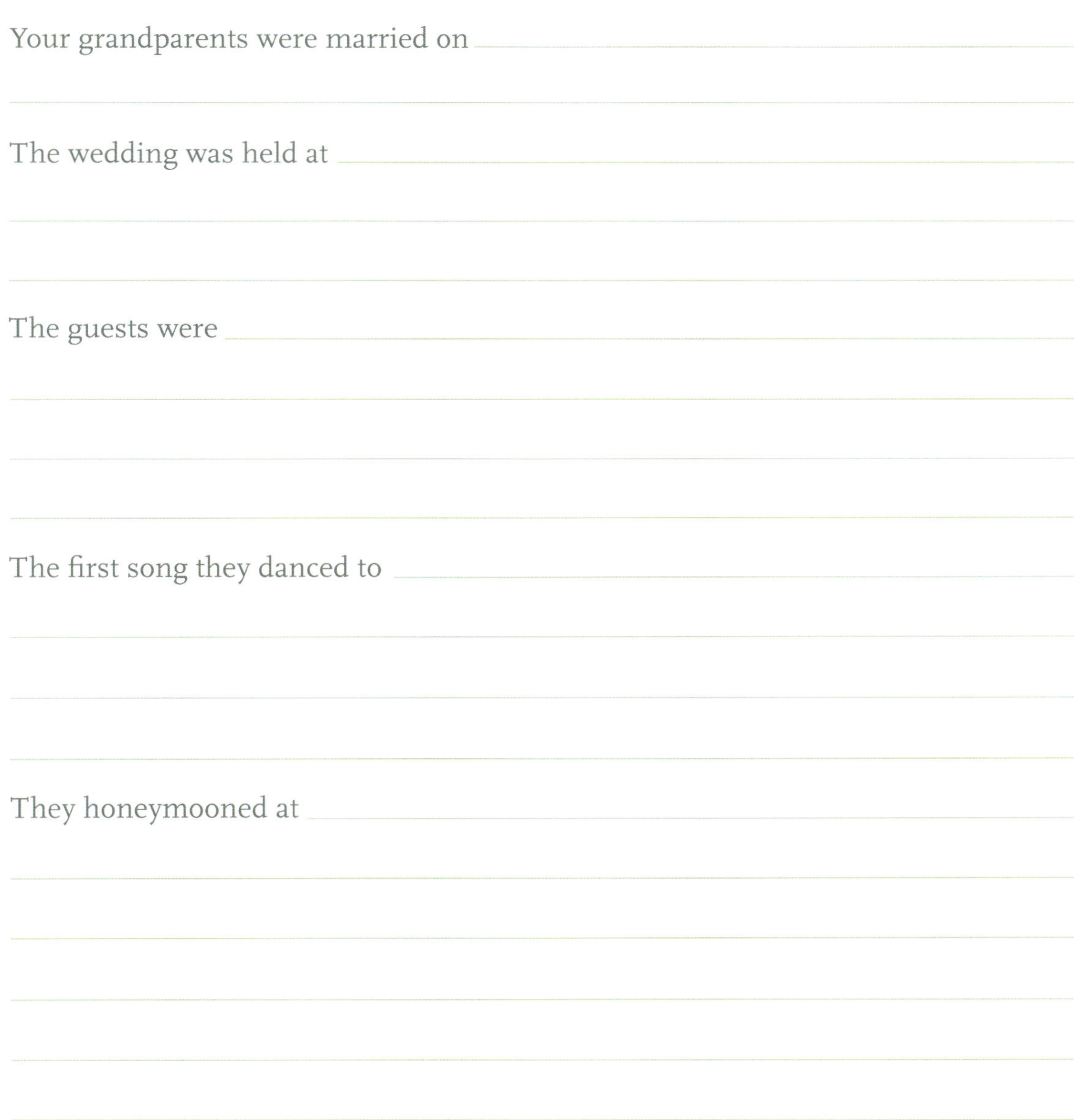

Your grandparents were married on

The wedding was held at

The guests were

The first song they danced to

They honeymooned at

Their Early Years Together

The location of their first home was

They chose that location because

Your grandmother worked at

Your grandfather worked at

Family meals were prepared by

A favorite meal was

They liked to vacation at

Their favorite pastime was

There were so many problems,
Even more than a few,
But they handled them all,
They knew just what to do.

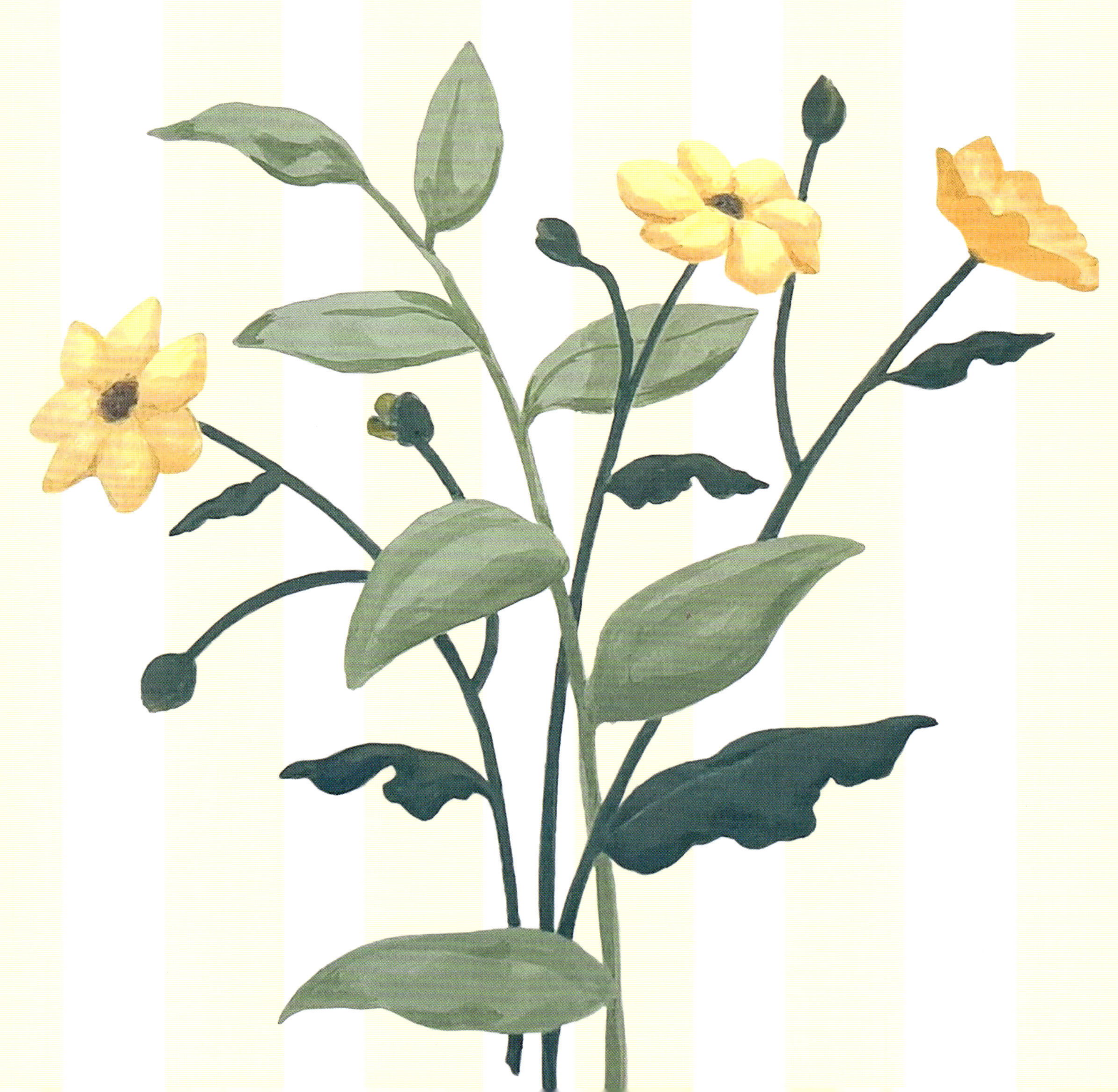

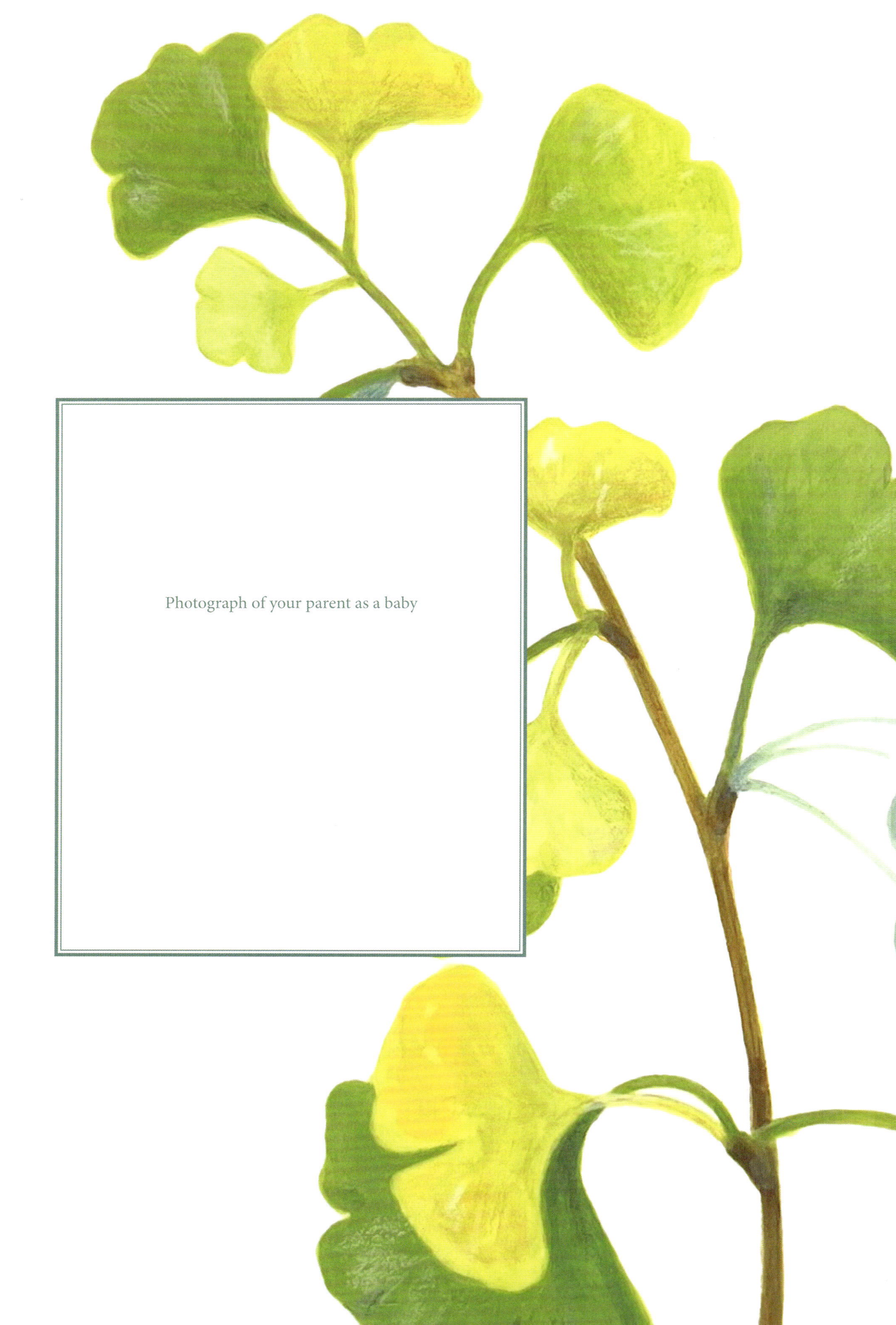

Photograph of your parent as a baby

The Birth of Your Parent

When your parent was born,
Everyone went wild,
There was such happiness,
We had a grandchild.

Your parent was born on

Your parent's birthplace was

Their given name

Their name was chosen because

We celebrated by

My wish for the new baby's future was

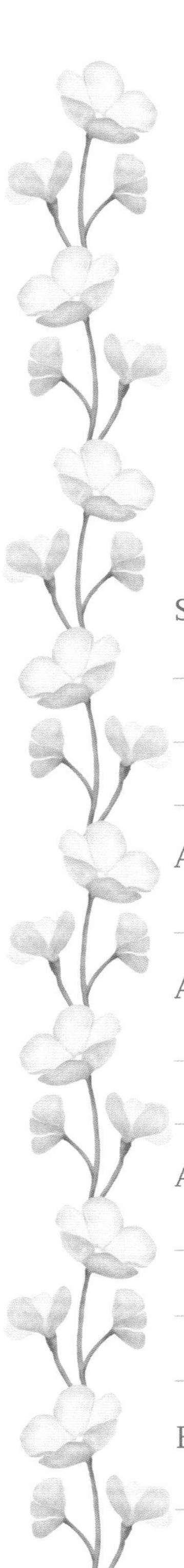

Your Parent's Growing-Up Years

When I was young and went to school,
Our homework was done by hand,
We now have computers and WiFi,
And there's lots to understand.

Schools attended were ______

After high school it was on to ______

Ambitions were ______

A challenge was ______

Best friends were ______

The happiest time was when ______

Your Parents Met

When two hearts met,
There was love in the air,
They had found each other,
And they were a devoted pair.

Your parents met

Their ages at the time were

Their education was

Their hopes and plans were

There never was a prettier bride,
And a handsome groom, that's true,
Everyone had a wonderful time,
And the food was delicious, too.

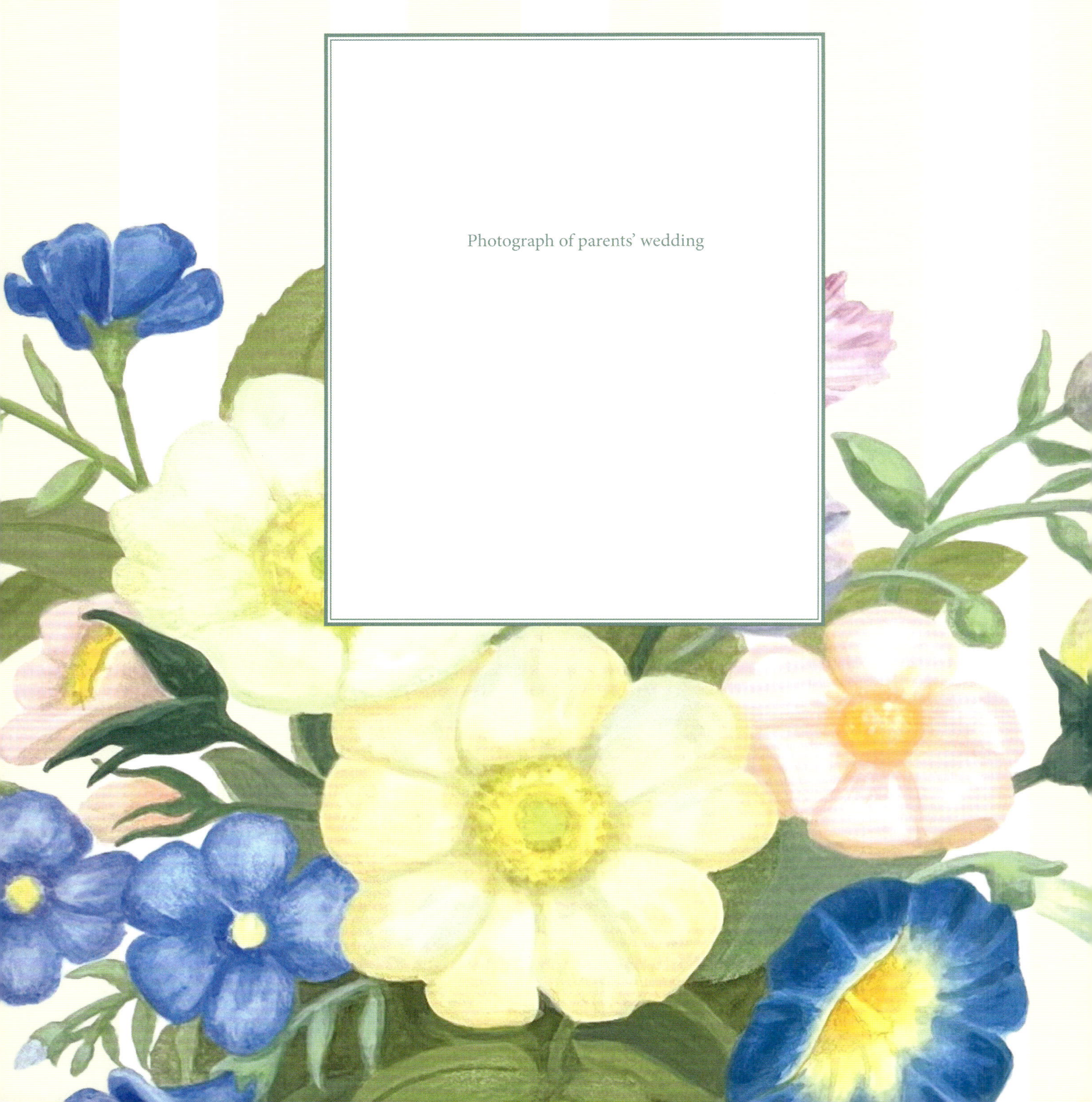

Photograph of parents' wedding

Your Parents' Wedding

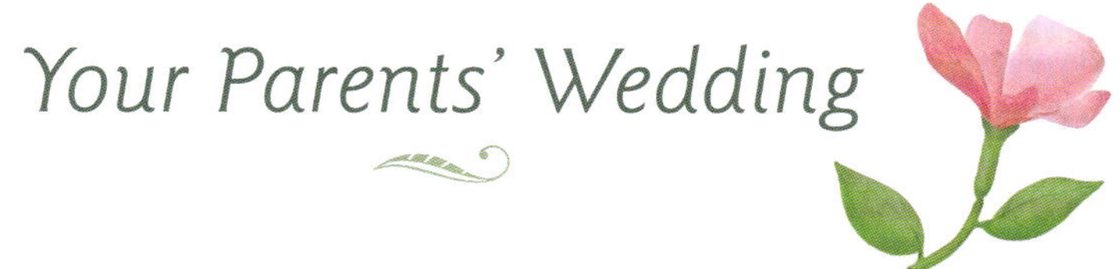

Date of the wedding ______________________

____

It was held at ______________________

____

____

The Maid of Honor ______________________

____

The Best Man ______________________

____

The vows were officiated by ______________________

____

____

The guests were ______________________

____

____

____

____

The Best Man toasted them by saying ______________________

____

____

____

____

____

____

Stories of Their Early Years

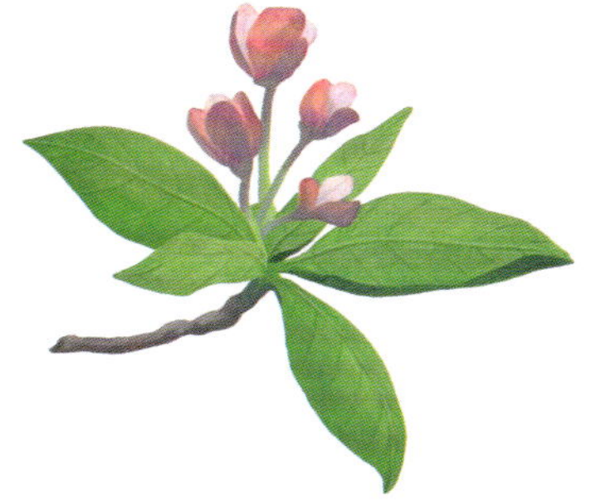

When marriage begins,
There's much to get done,
Balance a budget,
And leave time for fun.

Where they lived when first married

Your dad's job was

Your mom's job was

They saved up for

They vacationed at

A good story about them is

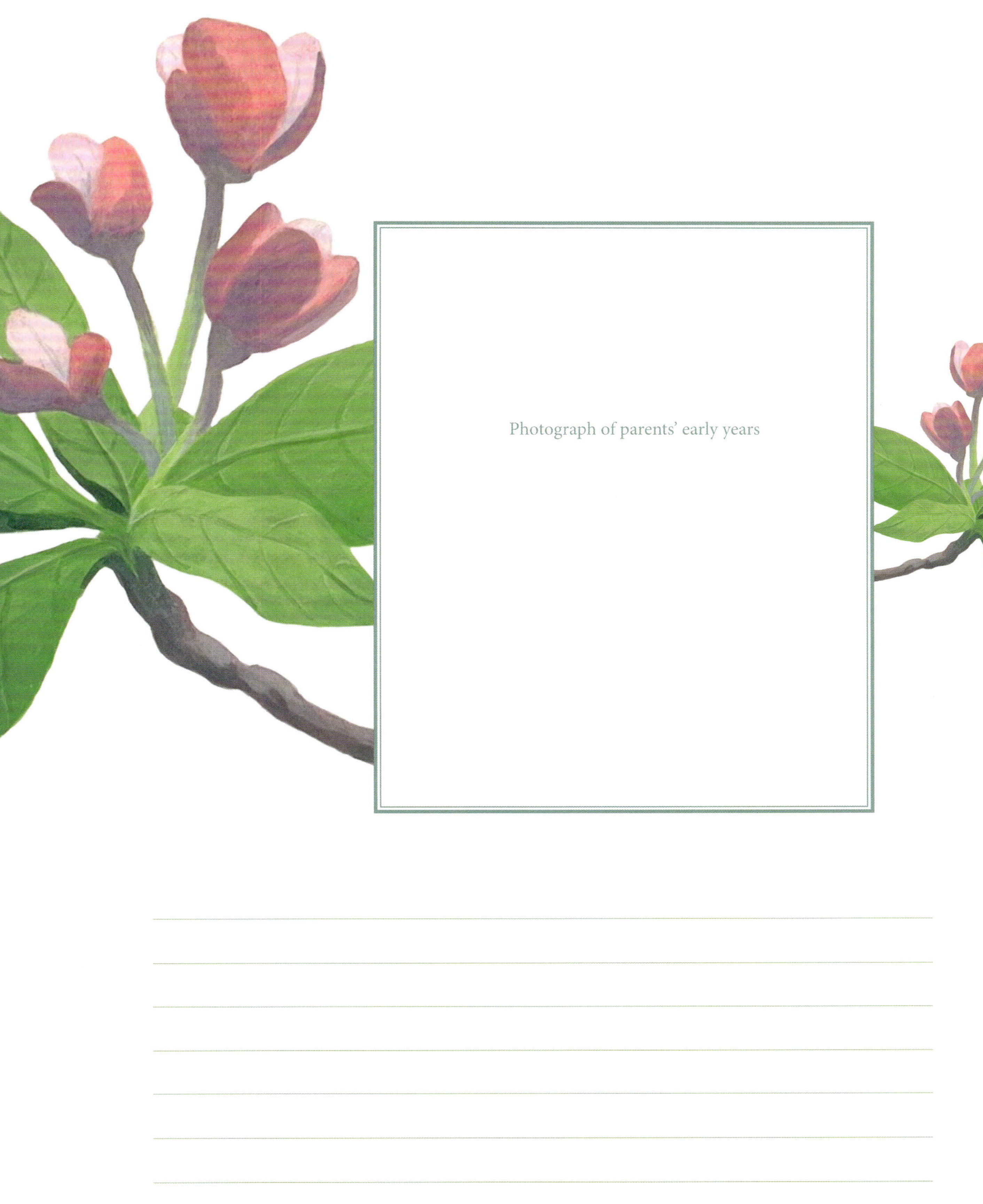

Photograph of parents' early years

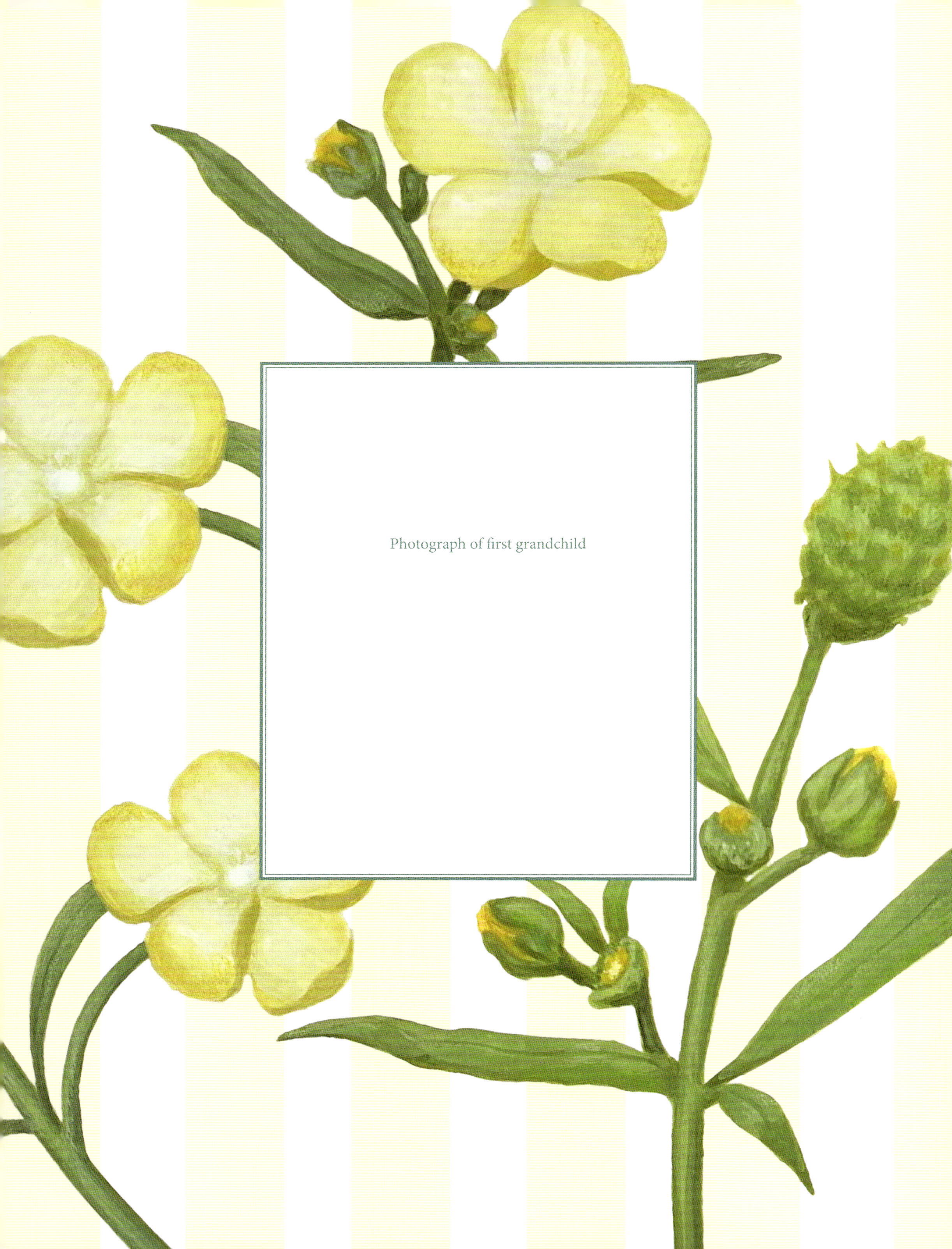

Photograph of first grandchild

My First Grandchild

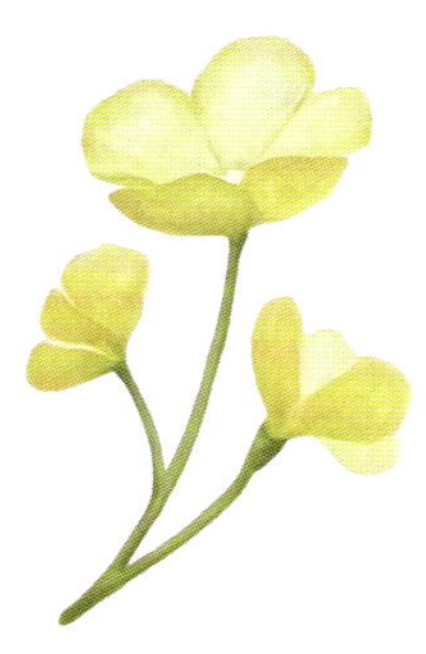

What a wonderful moment,
I was ecstatically wild,
When I was told,
I'd have a grandchild.

When I first heard the news, I ______________________________

____

____

I wanted to buy the baby ______________________________

____

____

I was counting the moments till ______________________________

____

____

They named the baby ______________________________

____

____

They chose this name because ______________________________

____

____

The first time I held my grandchild, I ______________________________

____

____

____

My Grandchild's Early Years

First the crawling, then the walking,
Each stage a miracle to see,
Now I was a grandmother,
And as happy as I could be.

Things I loved to see my grandchild do

Favorite foods were

Favorite baby books

Favorite toys

Bedtime was always

My Grandchild Went to School

So many things have happened,
I never expected to see,
The world has changed so fast,
Now it's all family history.

Preschool attended was

Grade school and high school attended were

After high school, they went to

My hopes for them were

An occasion that made me proud of you was

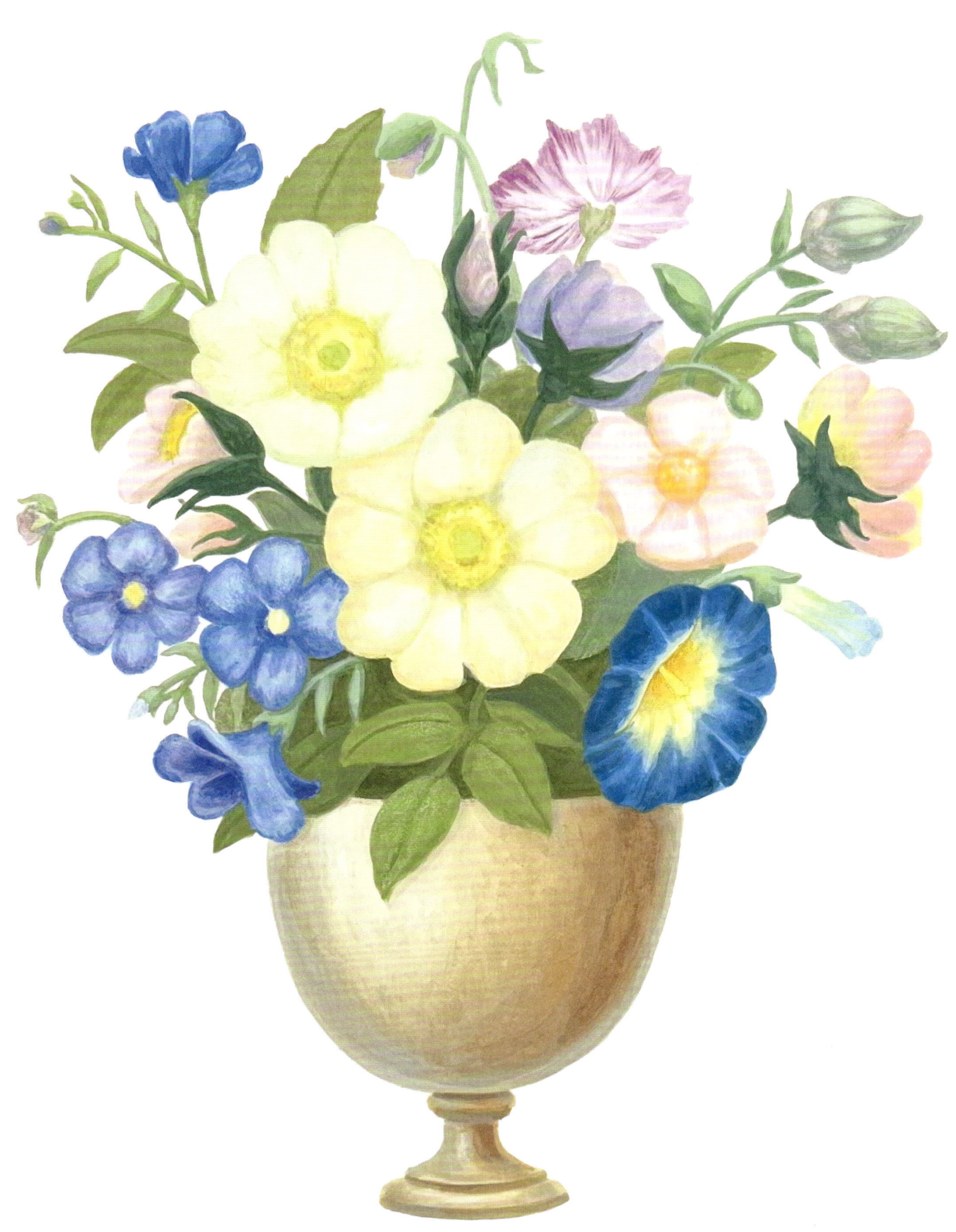

My Grandchild Met Their Beloved

They are so much in love,
Such a perfect pair,
They belong together,
Here and everywhere.

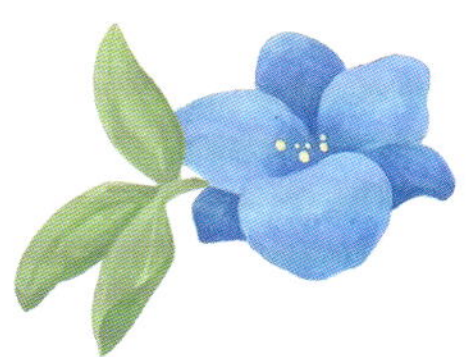

They met at ______________________________

____

____

They dated for ______________________________

____

____

Places they liked to go ______________________________

____

____

He worked at ______________________________

____

She worked at ______________________________

____

They both wanted to ______________________________

____

____

They made plans for ______________________________

____

____

____

They Become a Couple

It's wonderful to see,
A couple as happy as they,
Caring for each other,
In each and every way.

My grandchild became one half of a couple on ______________________________

____

Their first residence was ______________________________

____

____

They made plans to ______________________________

____

____

The future seemed bright because ______________________________

____

____

____

I was happy for them because ______________________________

____

____

____

____

____

____

____

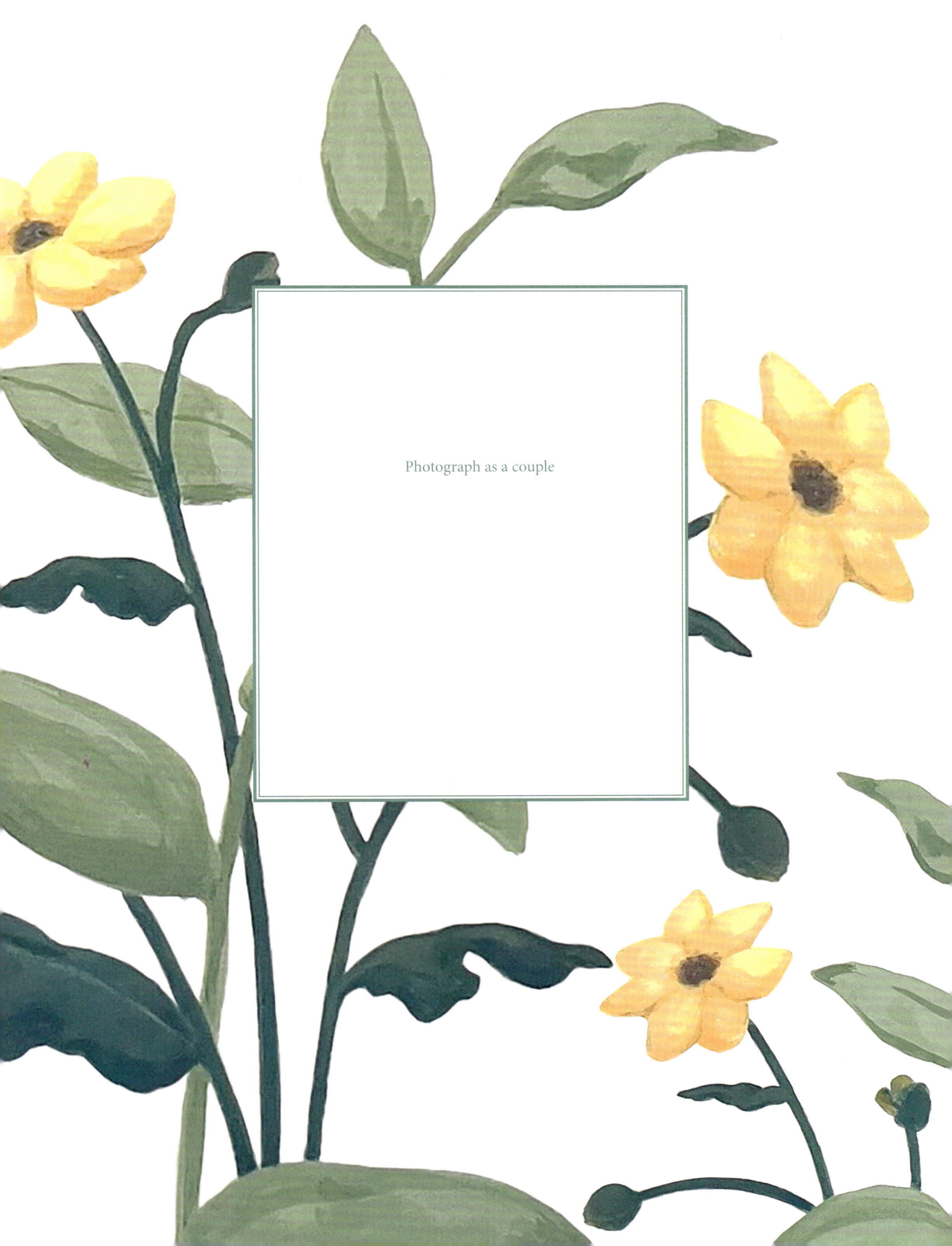
Photograph as a couple

What do I treasure?
Nothing of silver or gold,
Just this precious little baby,
I'm lucky enough to hold.

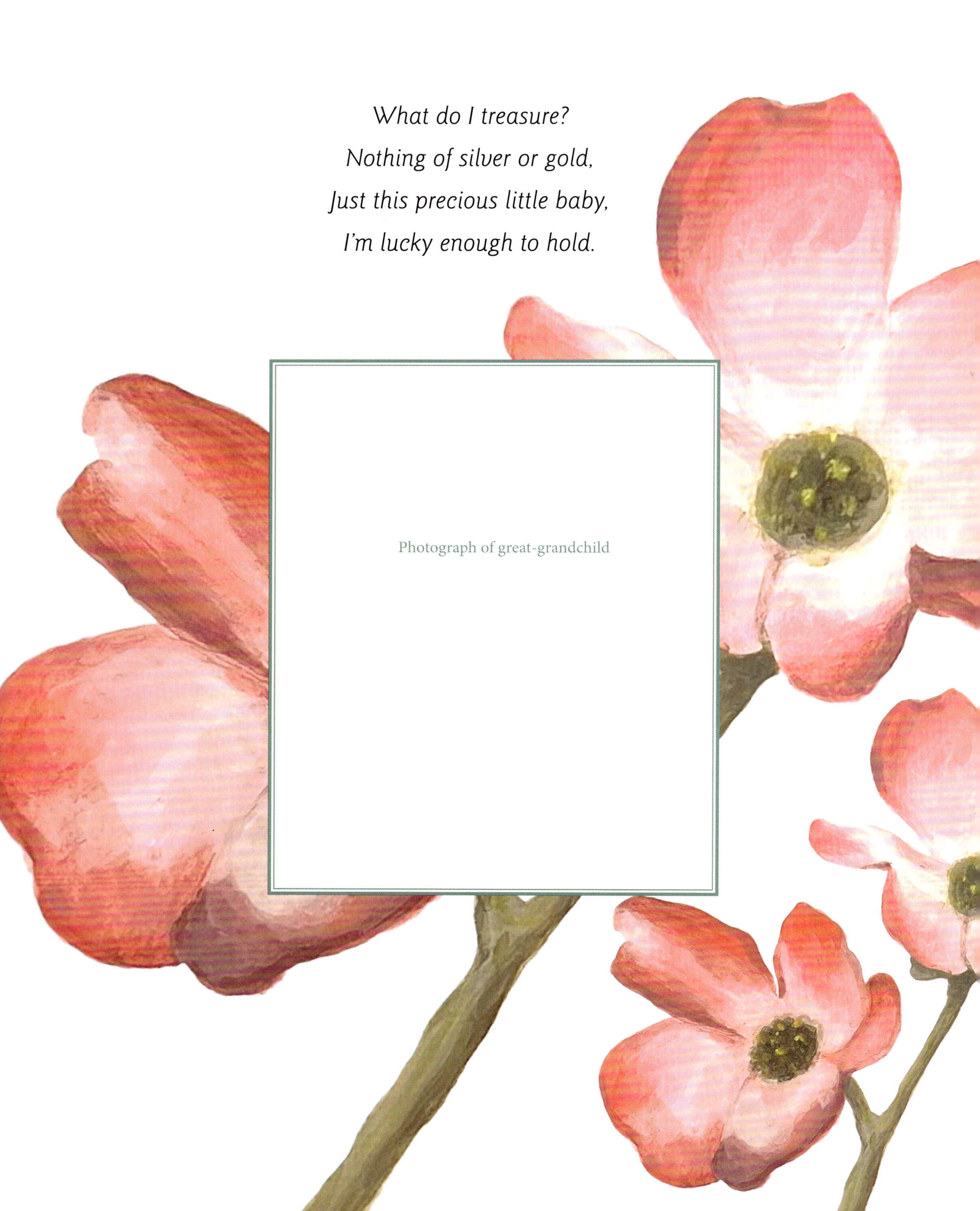

My Great-Grandchild Was Born

My great-grandchild was born on

Place of birth

Weight

The baby was named

My great-grandchild's name was chosen because

I'm the happiest great-grandmother in the world because

Other Members of Our Family

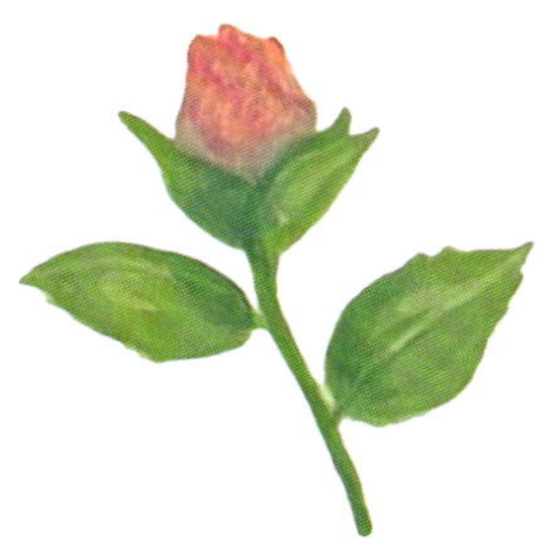

We have uncles and aunts,
And some cousins, too,
All eager to be invited,
And delight in meeting you.

The eldest members of our family are ______________________

____

____

____

They live at ______________________

____

Things that always make us laugh when we see each other ______________________

____

____

____

____

Family stories we like to remember are ______________________

____

____

____

____

____

I love our family because ______________________

____

____

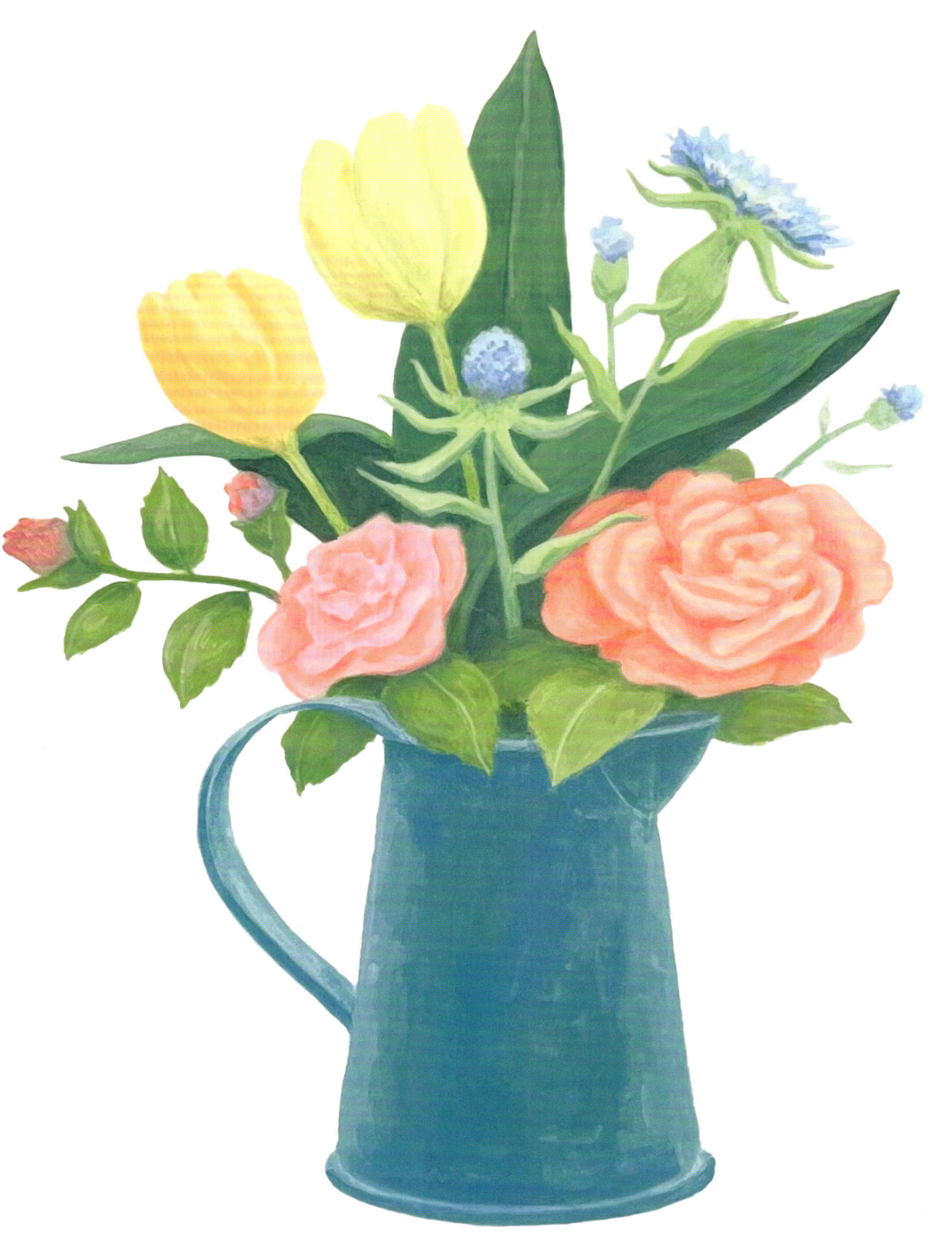

Great-Grandmother's Recipes

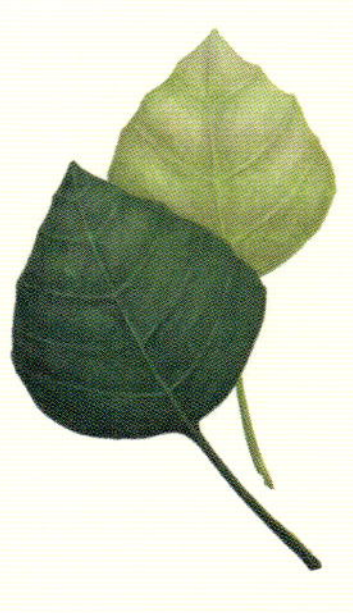

At holiday time we gathered,
And my family made me feel,
How much they loved sharing,
A delicious home-cooked meal.

Here is a recipe for

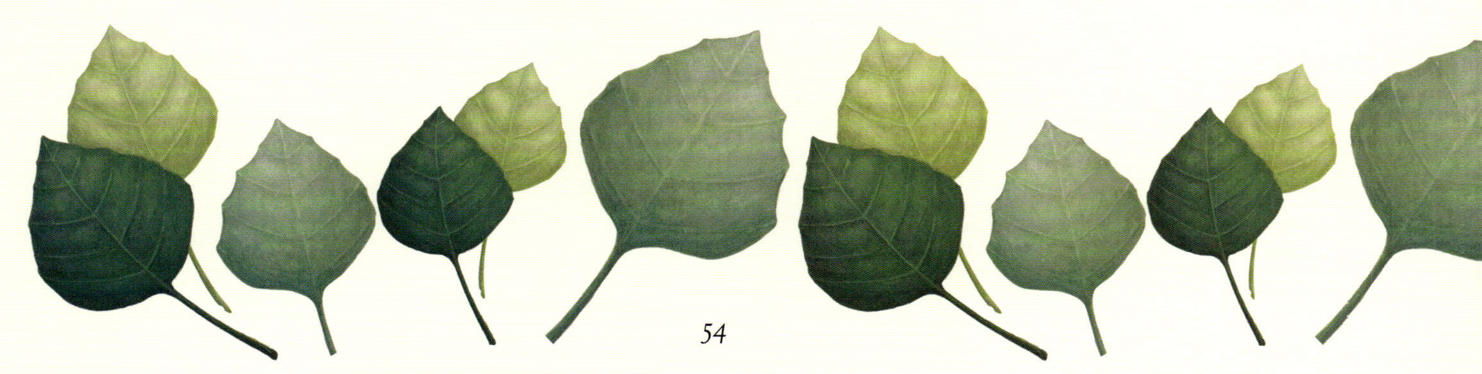

A family favorite dish was

Great-grandpa always loved

Great-Grandmother's Words of Wisdom

No one ever knows,
What the future will hold
So, get a good education,
Be strong, be right, be bold!

A good way to start your day is

Always remember

Always be kind to everyone, especially when

Try to save your money because

Be sure to use some funds for fun because

Let your word be something everyone can trust because

I Forgot to Mention

Life brought many surprises,
More than a few,
Here's some family history,
I'd like to share with you.

What has surprised me is

Something you probably don't know is

When I brag about you, I always say

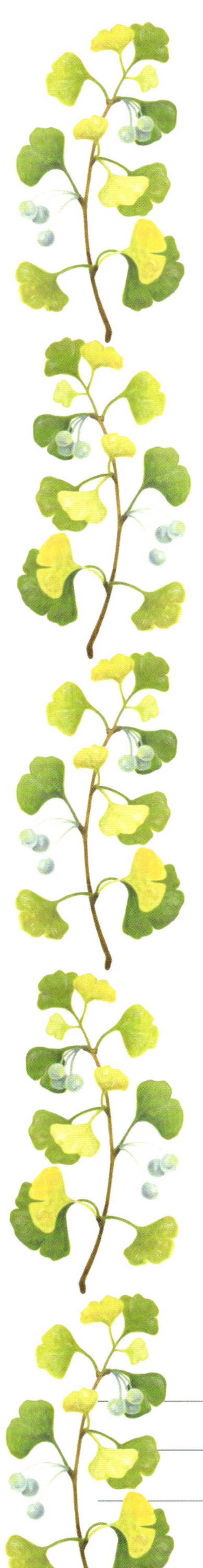

Gallery of Love

Here are pictures,
Of people you need to know,
They are family members,
Folks who love you so.

(Photos of family members with captions below)

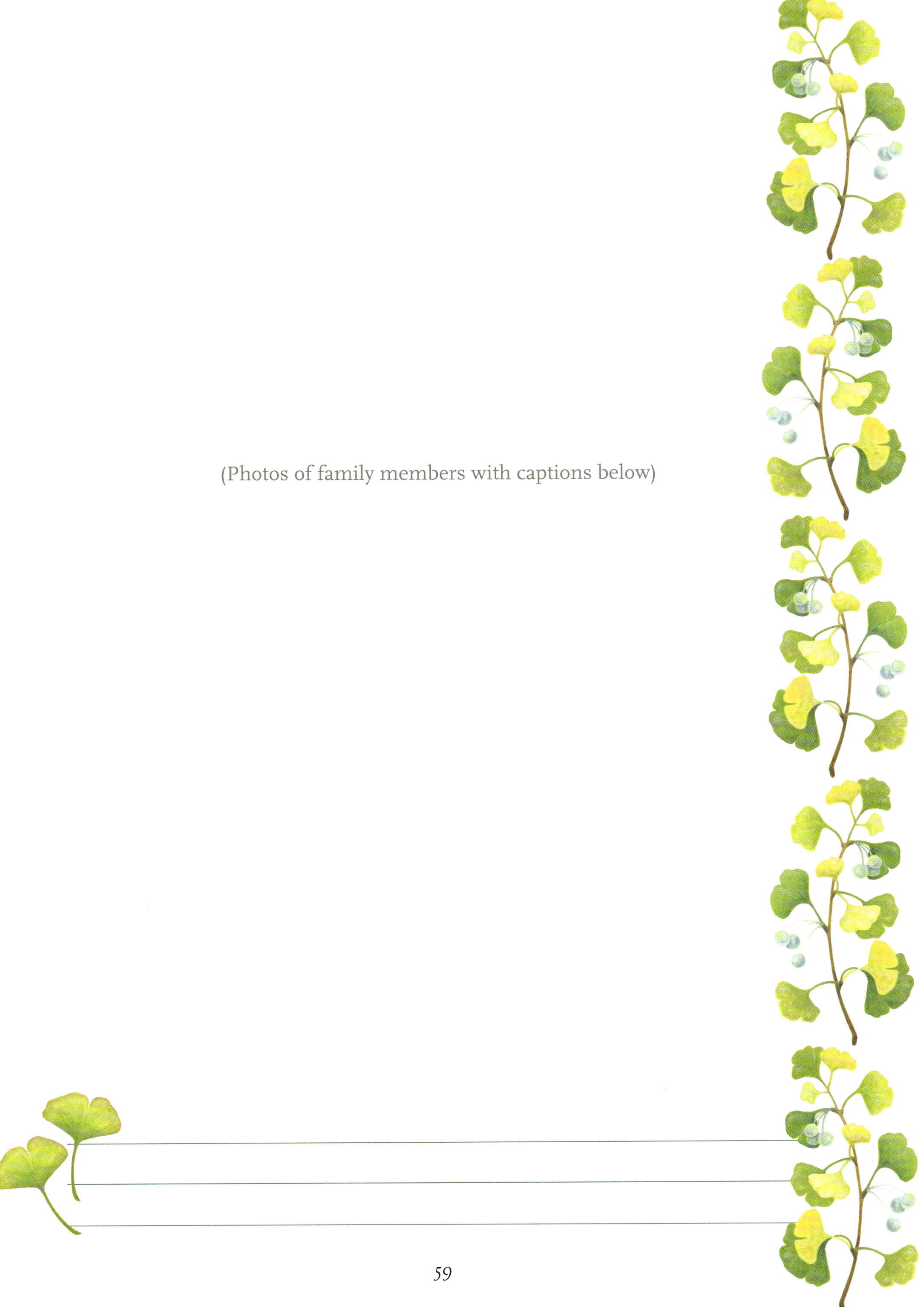

(Photos of family members with captions below)

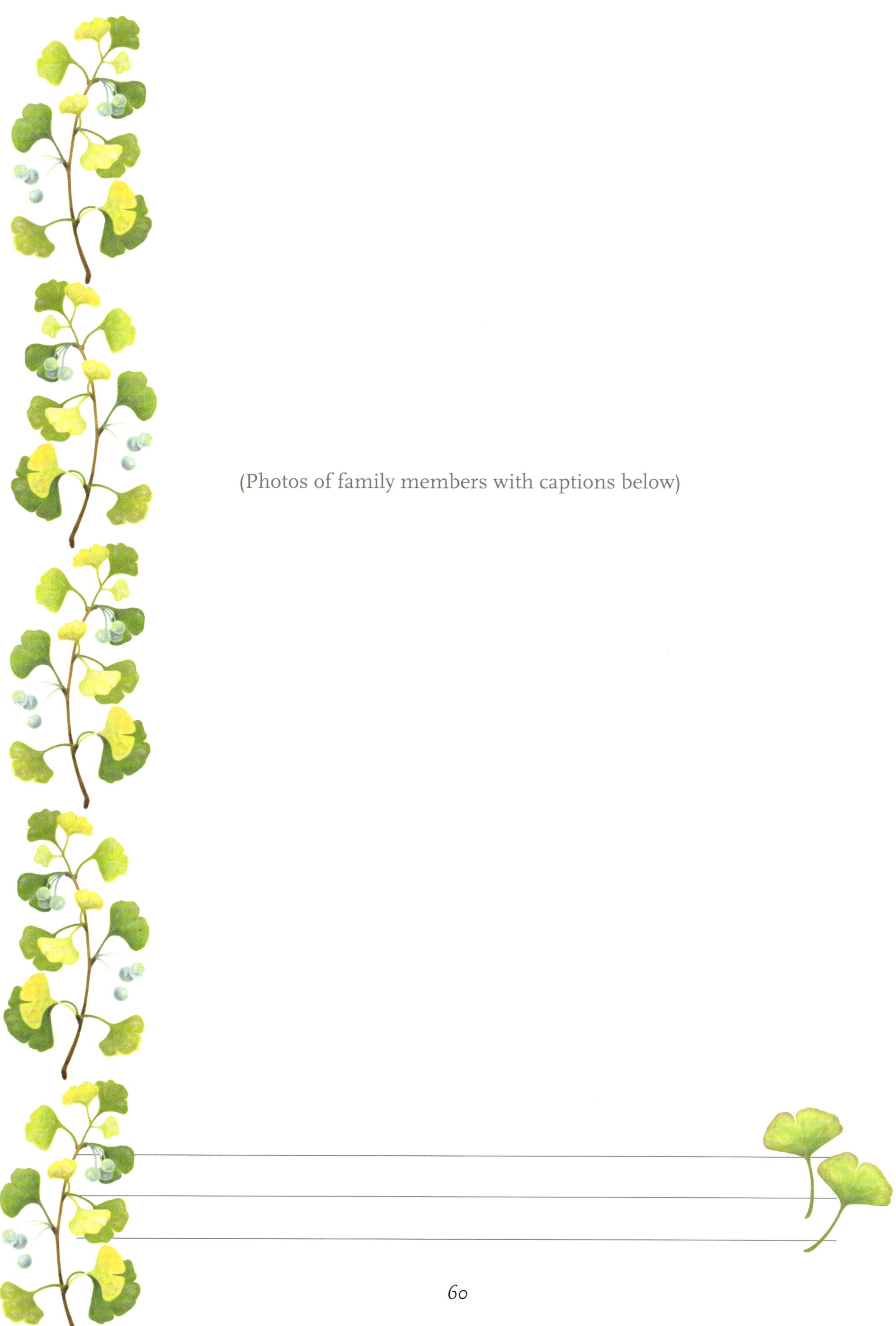

(Photos of family members with captions below)

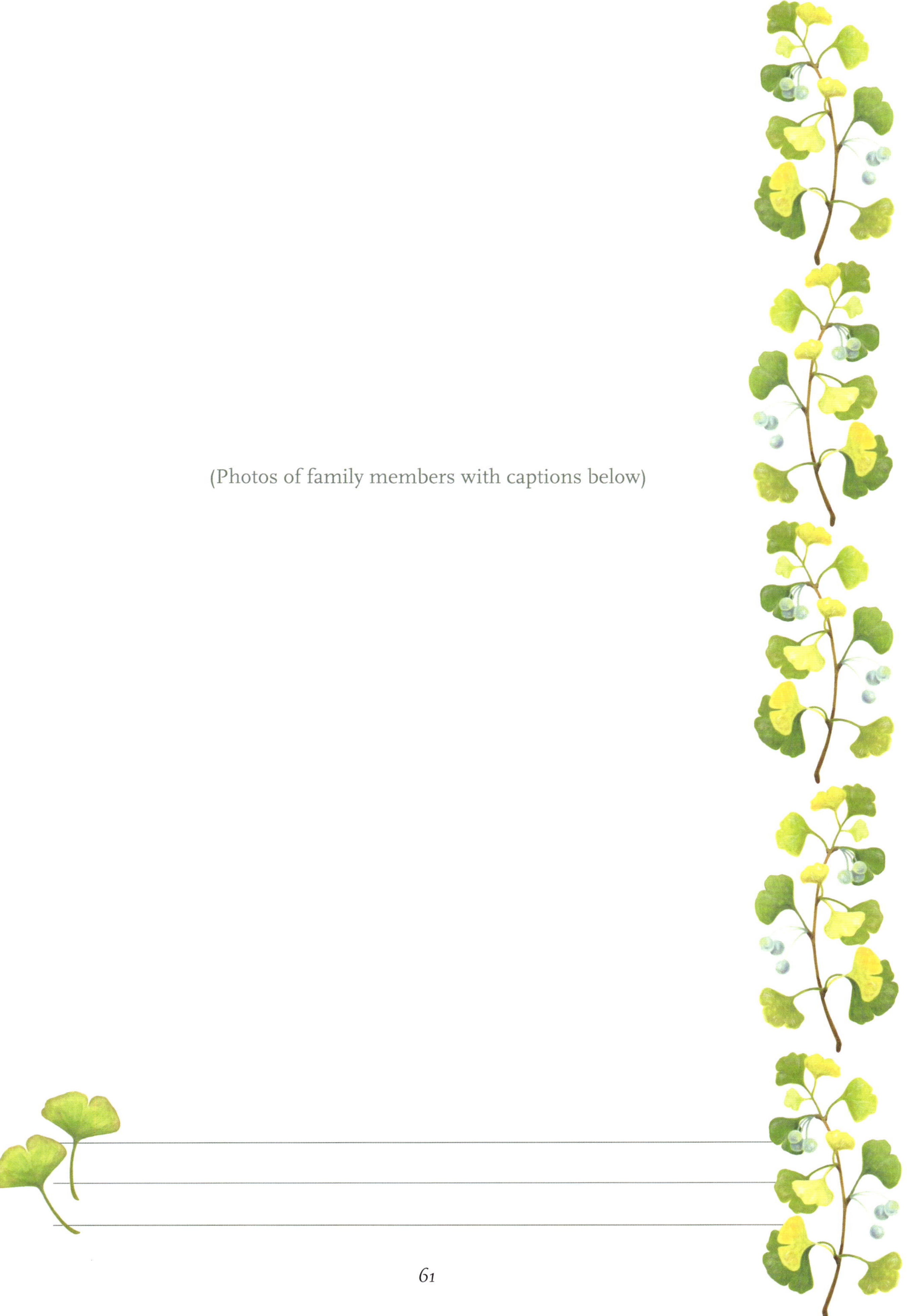

(Photos of family members with captions below)

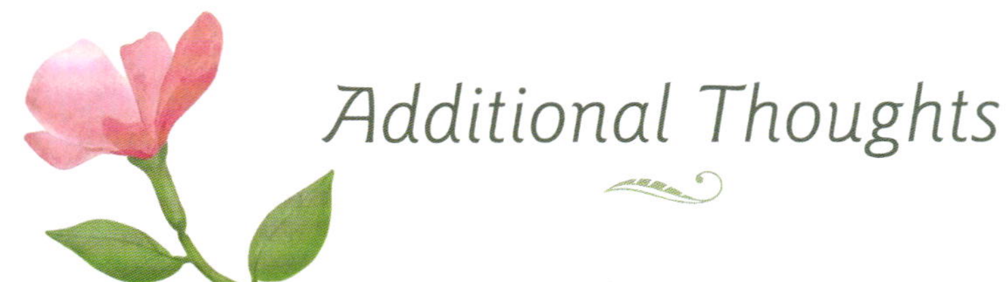

Additional Thoughts

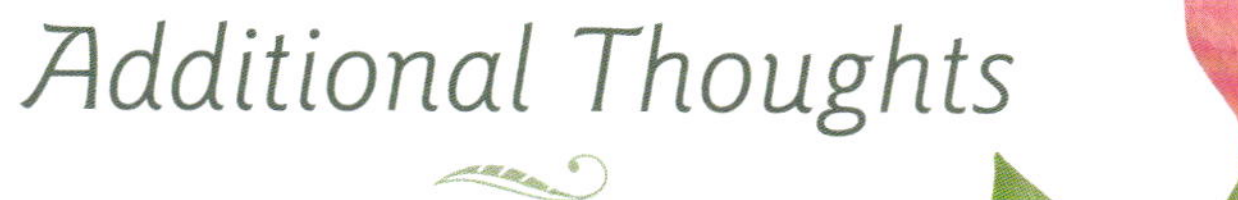

Additional Thoughts

Other books by Judith Levy:

Grandmother Remembers Holidays

Dad Remembers

Grandfather Remembers

Grandmother Remembers Songbook

Mom Remembers

Grandmother Remembers Family Recipes

Grandmother Remembers, 30th Anniversary Edition

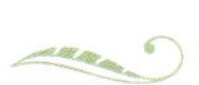

About the Author

Judith Levy is the author of more than ten family recordkeepers and lives today in Florida with her husband.

About the Illustrator

Artist and Illustrator **Noelle Giddings**'s work has been in galleries, television, comic books, and graphic novels. Her pictures for this book were created in her studios in Manhattan and Sag Harbor.